Local Flavor

JEAN IVERSEN

Local Flavor

Restaurants
That Shaped
Chicago's
Neighborhoods

Northwestern University Press
Evanston, Illinois

Northwestern University Press
www.nupress.northwestern.edu

The takeout container photo on page 17 is reproduced courtesy of WestRock Company. All other photos were taken by the author or Dino Robinson, production manager at Northwestern University Press, or are reproduced with permission from private collections.

The recipes on pp. 86–87 are reprinted with permission from Camille Stagg, *The Parthenon Cookbook: Great Mediterranean Recipes from the Heart of Chicago's Greektown* (Evanston, Ill.: Agate Surrey, 2008).

10 9 8 7 6 5 4 3 2 1

Library of Congress Cataloging-in-Publication Data
Names: Iversen, Jean, author.
Title: Local flavor : restaurants that shaped Chicago's neighborhoods / Jean Iversen.
Description: Evanston, Illinois : Northwestern University Press, 2018. | Includes bibliographical references.
Identifiers: LCCN 2017056200 | ISBN 9780810136717 (pbk. : alk. paper) | ISBN 9780810136724 (ebook)
Subjects: LCSH: Restaurants—Illinois—Chicago—History. | Ethnic restaurants—Illinois—Chicago—History. | Ethnic neighborhoods—Illinois—Chicago—History. | Chicago (Ill.)—History.
Classification: LCC TX909.2.I32 C455 2018 | DDC 647.9577311—dc23
LC record available at https://lccn.loc.gov/2017056200

To my mother, Marie, who lovingly documented the histories, recipes, and memories of the Iversen and Lammel families. Throughout her life, she shared with me her stories of growing up on the Northwest Side of Chicago, where she lived before moving to the Northwest suburbs in the 1950s to raise our family. After I moved to the city in the late 1980s, I regaled her with my adventures in Chicago. We would marvel at the vast differences in our respective experiences, both good and bad. I treasure each and every memory of her, from our lengthy discussions about Chicago history to the home-cooked meals she provided to us eight kids over many, many years. Her love and devotion to family inspired this book, and her spirit carried me through some of the more challenging moments while writing it. We would have had a ball talking about the people and places I've tried to capture in these pages. I dedicate this work to her with all my heart and in honor of her memory.

CONTENTS

INTRODUCTION

My first book, *BYOB Chicago*, was written over many conversations with the hundreds of restaurateurs who own Chicago's BYOBs, or bring-your-own-bottle restaurants. I noticed that many of the restaurant owners I talked to had something in common other than the lack of a liquor license: they were immigrants whose restaurants helped shape Chicago's ethnic neighborhoods. As they shared with me their stories of immigrating to Chicago, the evolution of their neighborhoods, and the inspirations behind their menus, I knew that these stories deserved to be told, their recipes shared.

Local Flavor details the histories of several restaurants owned by families who immigrated to Chicago anywhere from thirty to more than one hundred years ago. Some left their homelands to flee hardship or oppression. Others simply sought better opportunities in America. Some of these restaurants are currently operated by a second, third, even fourth generation in the same family. They are all considered to be anchors, pillars, or mayors in their respective communities.

According to the 2010 U.S. Census, of the approximately 9.5 million residents in Chicagoland, 1.6 million, or 18.6 percent, are foreign born. Like the Steve Earle song says, we're "livin' in a city of immigrants." Except we need to change the words to: "livin' in a metropolitan area of immigrants."

Ethnic enclaves in the city of Chicago, once strong footholds of Polish, Italian, Korean, and other immigrant populations, still exist, though many are now confined primarily to commercial districts, as foreign-born immigrants and their descendants live in the increasingly diverse communities throughout the six counties that make up Chicago's metropolitan area. The Italian and Greek immigrant communities that initially settled on the Near West Side, for example, were largely displaced in the late 1950s, when the expressways and UIC campus were built. The Northwest Side's Polish community is now dispersed throughout Chicagoland, with the majority living in the suburbs. Even Chicago's Puerto Rican population, once concentrated in the Humboldt Park neighborhood, has moved to other areas of the city. Many immigrants who now come to Chicagoland are settling in the suburbs, attracted to the increasingly diverse metro area.

Chinatown is somewhat of an exception. Chinese immigrants, particularly Cantonese families, have lived in Chicago's Chinatown since 1912. Pilsen is another. Originally settled by Europeans, Pilsen became a port of entry for families from Mexico in the 1950s and grew into the strong, vibrant Mexican community that it is today. Some even say that being in Pilsen, centered at Eighteenth Street, Loomis, and Blue Island, is like being in Mexico City.

While I was writing this book, some of the restaurants I was profiling closed or, in Nuevo Léon's case, tragically burned in a fire. Through much soul searching and discussions with my publisher, we decided to stay the course and keep these stories in the book, as they certainly merit a chapter in Chicago's culinary history. They also illuminate the vulnerable nature of small, family-owned restaurants, even those that have operated successfully for decades.

All restaurants operate in extremely unpredictable environments, yet they are held to higher and higher standards by both professional critics and customers, who now have online platforms from which to post both positive and negative reviews. One late produce delivery, one short-staffed dinner shift, even one overcooked steak, can spell disaster for a small business struggling to make every customer happy, every meal memorable.

We also have more and more restaurants to choose from every day— 7,300 in Chicago, according to the City of Chicago's website. With so much competition and so much scrutiny, it's a major achievement for any restaurant to survive the first one or two years in business. What makes the restaurants in this book even more remarkable is that they have all celebrated thirty, forty, even eighty-plus years in business—and counting. A few of them accept only cash. Some operate without computers or liquor licenses. One doesn't even have a sign. They all serve fresh food, made from natural, unprocessed ingredients. These businesses fly in the face of the conventional wisdom that in order to succeed, we must change with the times. These places feel frozen in time. At these neighborhood institutions the dishes, recipes, and native languages are all well preserved.

If any conclusions can be drawn from this book, it is that people simply crave rituals. Eating out at the same place—where the same owners greet you by name, where the orange chicken always tastes the same, where the same server has worked for several generations of customers—becomes a cherished ritual that keeps us connected to our current and past neighborhoods, our old and new friends, and, for some, our native cultures. While writing this book, I heard the same things over and over: "My father knows everyone by name." "The recipes stay the same." We all experience major change throughout our lives, in our jobs, our homes, and our relationships. Turning to well-worn clichés, many of us rely on places like the neighborhood restaurants in this book to help provide consistency, to remind us of where we've come from and who we are today.

These are the stories of people who have touched my life and the lives of thousands, perhaps millions. People who have left their mark on Chicago with their delicious food and hospitality. They have introduced so many of us to cuisine that represents their culture, food we wouldn't be able to enjoy in Chicago if it hadn't been for their courage to make a new life in a new land. To me, ethnic neighborhood restaurants that stand the test of time and serve time-honored recipes are no less important than the religious and civic institutions that shape our communities. I felt it was time for them to tell their stories through their food, their histories, and above all, their words.

Cheers,
Jean Iversen

Local Flavor

One

WON KOW
The Old Guard of Chinatown

Chicago's Chinatown, centered at Cermak Road and Wentworth Avenue about two miles south of Chicago's Loop, was established in 1912. It is not just difficult to find a Chinese restaurant that has remained in the same family since this neighborhood was established—it is impossible. I did find, however, the longest continually operated Chinese restaurant in Chinatown: Won Kow.

Established in 1928 by the influential Moy family, Won Kow resides on the second floor of an iconic three-story structure at 2237 South Wentworth. On the ground floor, the Hoypoloi Gallery carries eclectic art. Offices are on the third. Guardian lions, also known as Foo dogs, stand watch at the building's entrance. The center of the building is flanked by pagoda-like towers.

Won Kow's three-part sign, likely the original, strains massive chains out front, advertising "Chinese Restaurant" and "Cocktails" in English and in Chinese characters. The façade hasn't changed much since the building was completed, also in 1928. It was designed by Michaelsen & Rognstad, the same architectural firm that designed the similarly ornate Pui Tak building across the street. The former headquarters of the On Leong Merchants Association, Pui Tak currently houses a social service agency run by the Chinese Christian Union Church. It is the only structure in Chinatown with landmark designation. Decorative tiles on Pui Tak's façade, created by the Teco Pottery Company in Crystal Lake, Illinois, boast an array of vibrant colors, from turquoise to mustard yellow to jade green (Bronson, Chiu, and Ho 2011).

The distinctive Won Kow and Pui Tak buildings serve as anchors to the northern portal of Chinatown's commercial district on Wentworth. The gateway over Wentworth at Cermak is inscribed with the Chinese characters for *tian xia wei gong* (public spiritedness rules the world). Signs along the street are in both traditional Chinese characters and in English.

Won Kow, which translates to "the whole world," is currently owned and operated by Peter Huey and his nephew, David Hoy. Peter and his

Gateway to Chinatown's commercial district on South Wentworth Avenue

now-late brother Robert purchased the building in 1970 from Ronald Moy, the original owner's son. The brothers initially leased Won Kow to a restaurateur also named Moy. ("A different Moy," says Peter.)

Peter's first job in the restaurant business, coincidentally, was serving tables at Won Kow, after he first moved to Chicago from Hong Kong in 1950 during the post–World War II immigration wave that boosted Chinatown's population. After a few months, he moved on to own and operate several restaurants in the Chicagoland area, including Jade East on Cermak. Though all of these ventures were successful, he had grown weary of the long, exhausting hours of restaurant life and didn't plan on operating another one. When he and Robert purchased Won Kow's building in 1970, they planned on being only landlords, not restaurateurs.

In the late 1980s, however, Won Kow's tenant left. "They didn't take care of it," Peter says. "They moved out, and I took over." Peter and Robert performed an extensive renovation of Won Kow's interior, which had remained untouched since 1928. They planned on selling after, but no offers came in. "Somebody says, 'How come you don't want to open?' I say, 'I don't want to open; I want to sell it,'" says Peter. "And then I talked to my brother, and I say, 'We might as well open it, and then try to sell it.' When I finish remodeling, almost 1990. So I open it up, and when I open up, then, you know, the business is good and doing well. So then we never mentioned about selling it. Soon enough, now I find out it's twenty-five years gone."

Now in his nineties, Peter still climbs the steep stairs up to the restaurant every morning to manage the dim sum and lunch shifts. Restaurant life seems to agree with Peter, who moves nimbly for a man in his tenth decade. Other than diabetes, which he says he manages with a restricted diet, he seems quite vibrant and healthy. A slow, sweet smile comes to his face easily. On most days, he is dressed in a sports jacket and dress pants, working in the tiny office near the entrance amid piles of paperwork and handwritten reservations tacked on the walls.

Peter's memory is as sharp as the chef's knives lined up like soldiers in the kitchen. But he doesn't realize what a treasure trove of memories he holds. Or, if he does, he is shy, almost embarrassed, to offer it. One day, I called Peter to ask if I could come in for one of our chats.

Sure, he said, come on in. Then, after a short pause, he asked, "You don't think you can find anybody better than me, huh?" After assuring him that he was indeed a valuable historian not only for Won Kow, but for Chicago's Chinatown, he relented. "I do what I can, that's all."

Since the late 1980s remodeling project, Won Kow's dining room hasn't changed much. The best seats in the house overlook South Wentworth Avenue from a bank of windows. Red paper lanterns advertising Tsingtao beer dangle from the ceiling. Wood paneling and brass railings give it a retro feel, while an enormous, backlit photo of Hong Kong's Kowloon Bay presides over a wall near the entrance. Like many lifelong restaurateurs, Peter seems happiest when working. "I don't have much to do, so I take care of it," he says of his charge, the slow, kind smile always at the ready. "If I give it up, I don't know what to do."

This Is a Moy Town

The vast majority of Chinese immigrants who first came to the United States were from the Toisan area of Guangdong Province in southern China, north of Hong Kong. When U.S. ships came to China to recruit cheap labor in the mid-1800s, Toisan was the district most accessible to the sea. Chinese workers first came to San Francisco, where they labored on western farms; served as miners, cooks, and laundrymen; and helped build the first transcontinental railroad, which was completed in 1869.

As more and more Chinese immigrants arrived, filling more and more jobs, anti-Chinese sentiment spread. Congress responded with the 1882 Chinese Exclusion Act, which restricted the number of Chinese workers in the United States and limited travel freedoms for those already living here. The act also prohibited Chinese women from entering the United States unless they were married to teachers, students, or business owners (Chinatown Museum Foundation 2005). This sentiment was particularly rampant in the western United States, causing many Chinese to take the new railroad and travel east, looking for acceptance and more job opportunities. As Chicago was a railroad terminus and major industrial center, many came to Chicago, where they started to establish the city's original Chinatown, centered on South Clark Street between Van Buren and Harrison streets.

Moy is the family name that dominates Chicago's Chinatown. The three original Moy brothers moved to Chicago from San Francisco in 1878, according to John Rohsenow, who taught Mandarin Chinese and linguistics at the University of Illinois for thirty years. "That's why most of the people in this town are named Moy," says Rohsenow, who is now on the board of directors of the Chinese-American Museum of Chicago. "This is a Moy town."

The Moys became Chinatown's largest and most influential family. They led the On Leong Merchants Association, one of two major Chinese merchant associations in Chicago. The other one, Hip Sing, is now headquartered at 1121 West Argyle Street in what some call Chicago's "North Chinatown." On Leong and Hip Sing are commonly described as rival Chinese merchant associations, or tongs. Both settled in Chicago's original Chinatown. When On Leong moved to the Pui Tak building in 1912, most of the Chinese merchants followed. Hip Sing stayed on South Clark Street until finally moving to Argyle in 1974, when it was displaced by the Metropolitan Correctional Center.

The Pui Tak building at 2216 South Wentworth Avenue

American Chinese Food

Nearly all of the Chinese immigrants who settled in Chicago before 1943, when the Exclusion Acts were repealed, came from the Toisan district. In fact, about 86 percent of Chinese Americans can trace their ancestry to Guangdong Province, mostly to the Toisan district (Rohsenow 2003, 322), which explains the proliferation of Cantonese restaurants throughout America in the twentieth century.

Back in the 1920s and 1930s, said Rohsenow, there were a "gazillion" Cantonese restaurants in Chicago. "They were famous for their dance bands. It was all Cantonese [people] and Cantonese food." These restaurants offered Cantonese food adapted for American tastes. Orange chicken and chop suey, which literally means "leftovers" in Cantonese, are dishes created in America for Americans. If you order these dishes in China, you may get a completely different dish. Or you may just get a blank stare. Peter hears it all the time: people go to China, order a certain dish, and Chinese chefs don't even know what it is. "They call it American Chinese food," he says.

Cantonese cuisine is not traditionally spicy. Spicy Chinese food, says Peter, is "mostly from the north." Peter added a spicy-dishes section to Won Kow's menu to accommodate Americans' growing taste for spicy fare. American Chinese food also reflects Americans' love for all things fried. Other than using a small amount of oil to stir-fry food, Peter claims, Chinese cooks "never use oil. Oil, in the old days, was very expensive. They steam everything. In this country," he added, "people like deep fried, they like fast food." Won Kow cooks with corn oil. "Used to be we used lard," Peter continued. "No more, because those are bad for heart. Now we use corn oil, vegetable oil . . ."

Throughout its history, Won Kow has held onto its menu of both authentic Cantonese and American Chinese cuisines. About 10 percent of the menu is devoted to American Chinese food, Peter estimated one day while we chatted. After scanning the menu further, he said "maybe 20 percent." I had the feeling that if he were to comb through every one of the 200 menu items one more time, the percentage would jump a bit higher.

Popular American Chinese dishes on Won Kow's menu include the chicken almond ding and cashew chicken, both a stir-fry of Chinese vegetables, roasted almonds or cashews, and chicken. Others are *gwen chow nau hor*, which is made with beef, bean sprouts, onions, and flat rice noodles, or *foon*; the Won Kow Special, a stir-fry of beef, chicken, shrimp, bean sprouts, and "other Chinese vegetables in a brown sauce"; and orange chicken.

"Orange chicken, that's a popular dish," says Peter, who always keeps one eye on the restaurant's entrance while he talks. "If you go to China, order that, probably they don't know how to do it," he continued. "But over here, the people eat it . . . they like it, they order it over and over. So it's just sort of American-style Chinese." What makes it orange? I asked Peter one morning before dim sum service while he sipped tea from his usual University of Illinois mug. "Orange juice," he replied. "They deep-fry the chicken and cut it up, put the sauce on top."

The remainder of the menu reflects authentic Cantonese cuisine, which is primarily seafood based, as Guangdong, like Hong Kong, borders the South China Sea. Regulars turn to Won Kow's fried oysters, Dungeness crab, and fish *kow*, a pan-fried pike with stir-fried Chinese vegetables. Peking duck is also "a typical Chinese dish," Peter explains, "not an American creation." Some Chinese restaurants just serve the duck skin, fried to a delicate crisp. Won Kow serves the breast, a broth made with the bones, and the fried skin, along with pancake wrappers, scallions, and hoisin sauce. Duck is a huge seller at the restaurant, Peter exclaims. "Oh, we sell a *lot*! Half or the whole duck. A lot of Peking duck. Americans, too. Oh—European people love ducks! They order the duck a lot."

Won Kow's business has suffered from the competition down the street, which offers faster service and other styles of Chinese food, such as spicier Sichuan. But all of Won Kow's food is made to order, Peter says. Even the pot stickers and dumplings, typically bought frozen at other places, are made to order every day. Won Kow uses four cooks—most of them trained in Hong Kong—to prepare every single dish that comes out of its spacious, immaculate kitchen. "When you order, they start picking out all the ingredients and put it together. It's fresh," Peter boasted. It's more expensive, he says, but it's the only way Peter knows how to run a restaurant—by serving delicious food made from scratch.

Old Guard versus New Guard

Cermak Avenue cuts through the middle of Chinatown and serves as the unofficial cultural divide between old and new development. Turn south under the arch onto Wentworth, and you'll encounter Chinatown's old guard: Won Kow, the Pui Tak building, and the Chinese Christian Union Church. The iconic Amtrak lift bridge on Canal, completed in 1915, looms in the distance along the Chicago River, where Chinatown's dragon boat races launch every summer. The Canal Street Marina buzzes with activity in Chicago's precious warmer months. Turn north on Wentworth from Cermak, and you'll see the new guard: Chinatown Square, a pedestrian mall designed by Chicago architect Harry Weese that replaced the old Santa Fe railroad switchyards in 1993; the tranquil Ping Tom Memorial Park; and an ultramodern Chicago Public Library building designed by Skidmore, Owings, & Merrill that opened in 2015. New-guard eateries offering bubble teas, hot pots, and other styles of Asian food compete more and more for customers that once crowded Cantonese restaurants like Won Kow.

There are myriad reasons for this seismic shift in Chicago's Chinatown. Joyce Chen, a celebrated Chinese chef, restaurateur, entrepreneur, and author, was one of the first to bring authentic Chinese cuisine to America. "She was the one who started getting people to cook Chinese food at home," says Rohsenow. Chen came to Cambridge, Massachusetts, from Peking in 1949. After discovering a passion and talent for cooking authentic Chinese food for the local academic community, Chen opened her own restaurant in Cambridge in 1958. Her desire, she said, was "to open a Chinese restaurant which would make American customers happy and Chinese customers proud . . . not only a place to enjoy truly authentic Chinese food, but . . . a cultural exchange center" (Chen 1962, 3).

The Joyce Chen Cook Book, published in 1962, was written for those who didn't have access to an authentic Chinese restaurant. It introduced Americans to Mandarin, Shanghai, and other styles of Chinese food. It was difficult at the time to obtain Chinese ingredients. Most big cities in the United States had Chinatowns, but not all, so ingredients had to be imported from Taiwan or Hong Kong. And authentic Chinese recipes weren't available in America. *The Joyce Chen Cook*

Book filled that gap and brought authentic, but accessible, Chinese recipes to the American home cook. Chen died in 1994; her quintessential cookbooks remain classics for chefs and home cooks throughout the world.

When Chen first arrived on the scene, Americans didn't cook *any* Chinese food at home; they had thousands of Cantonese restaurants from which to choose around the country. And Chinese restaurants in America offered only Cantonese food until about 1972, when Nixon made his historic visit to China. "When Nixon went to China, suddenly Chinese food exploded," says Rohsenow, referring to all types of Chinese food, or what are known as China's eight culinary traditions: Cantonese, Sichuan, Jiangsu, Zhejiang, Fujian, Hunan, Anhui, and Shandong. "Before that, there were bad Cantonese restaurants all over the country. You know what I'm talking about? In every town. There's one on Route 16 on the road to New Hampshire near my parent's house. Cantonese restaurants . . . adapted to American taste."

In 1979, the United States restored diplomatic relations with China. It became legal to import goods directly from the mainland. Rohsenow, who was teaching Mandarin at UIC at the time, recalls some turbulence as Chinese restaurateurs began importing foodstuffs from mainland China and serving it in Chicago. One particular Chinatown restaurant, he remembers, "got their windows busted out, because there were so many anticommunist people here. It took a while." Now, says Rohsenow, the waters are calm, and at least half the Chinese businesses in Chicago import their goods from China proper. "But in the beginning, there was a lot of political division between those supporting Taiwan and those willing to reconcile with the People's Republic."

Since then, the barriers to goods imported from China have largely disappeared, and Chinatown's grocery stores and restaurants have easy access through local suppliers (Lee 2015). Chinese wholesalers started to appear in Chicago sometime in the 1990s, says Peter. He gets all of his vegetables—including Chinese vegetables—from domestic sources. He only imports canned goods from China. Meats are purchased in Chicago or other parts of the United States. Even Won Kow's almond and fortune cookies are sourced locally from Golden Country at 2355 South Blue Island.

Chinatown's new guard is synonymous with the name Tony Hu. Since 1998, with the opening of his flagship restaurant, Lao Sze Chuan at 2172 South Archer in Chinatown Square, Hu's mission has been to bring what he calls "real" Chinese cuisine to America. Unlike cuisine that represents the various regions of Europe, regional Chinese cuisine hasn't quite gained a foothold in America. Judging from our long love affair with fried, sweet American Chinese food, I'd say it's a mistrust of American tastes—an assumption our palates would simply reject "real" Chinese food. Hu aims to reverse this assumption, one plate at a time.

Hu's company, Tony Gourmet Group, has opened several restaurants throughout Chinatown, other parts of Chicagoland, and cities such as Las Vegas and Los Angeles. All operate under the Lao (which translates to old) brand and represent the cuisines from several of China's regions, from Lao Sze Chuan to Lao Shanghai to Lao Hunan. Chicago's Lao Sze Chuan has been named a Bib Gourmand selection by Michelin, and Hu has received accolades from both American and Chinese organizations for his culinary achievements and community involvement.

Starting in 2012, Hu came under investigation for tax fraud. He was eventually charged with tax fraud–related crimes and sentenced to prison in 2016. The long-term fallout from Hu's legal battles have yet to unfold. But it's clear that the future culinary ambitions of "the mayor of Chinatown" in Chicago and beyond are uncertain.

The Singapore Sling: "You'll Swear You Were There"

The tradition of serving American Chinese food alongside tiki drinks—and vice versa—goes back to the first Don the Beachcomber Café, which opened in Hollywood in 1933. Owner Ernest Gantt, who changed his name to Donn Beach, added Cantonese food to his menu in 1937 after moving to a larger location with a kitchen. A Don the Beachcomber location opened at 101 East Walton Place in Chicago in 1940 and also served American Chinese food. Another tiki bar, Trader Vic's, also had locations in California and Chicago. Legend has it that Trader

Vic's founder, Vic Bergeron, created the mai tai in 1944 in Oakland, California. By the mid 1950s, Trader Vic's was also serving Cantonese food alongside fruity rum drinks (Spiers 2015, Loring 1970).

Though Won Kow's sign boldly advertises "cocktails," Peter doesn't recall serving tiki drinks during his brief stint as a server at Won Kow in 1950—only spirits such as whiskey. A Won Kow menu dated 1933 that Peter found in the building's basement reveals that the restaurant served only soda, milk, and coffee at the time. Won Kow's tropical drink menu was fully developed, however, by the time Peter and his brother bought the building in 1970. Peter's best guess of the year that Won Kow started serving tropical drinks is 1960. He adds that "Caucasians order these drinks. Not Chinese."

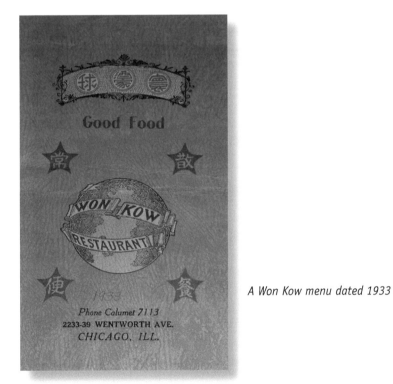

A Won Kow menu dated 1933

Won Kow offers standard umbrella-topped tipplers such as the Singapore sling and the zombie, a concoction made with four different kinds of alcohol. The menu includes kitschy descriptions after each drink, noting that "you'll swear you were there" when you order a Singapore sling, or that "George Romero couldn't do better" when sipping on a zombie. Won Kow is famous for its volcano version of these potent cocktails, which are served in large, colorful bowls and sipped communally from giant straws. Before they are served, David Hoy, who works the dinner shift and does double duty as bartender, floats a small cup of booze in the center and sets it aflame. For many regulars, no trip to Won Kow is complete without a volcano.

Dim Sum, or "Chinese Tapas"

Dim sum is a famous Chinese culinary tradition that originated in Guangdong Province. Traditionally served for breakfast, and now for brunch in America, dim sum is an assortment of sweet and savory *bao*, or buns; dumplings; rice noodle rolls; and other small-plate delicacies, which are either steamed or fried. Dim sum translates to "touch the heart" and is linked to the tradition of *yum cha*, or drinking tea (Gourse 1988).

"Three Happiness was the original dim sum restaurant," Rohsenow remembers, referring to one of Chinatown's oldest restaurants on Cermak near Wentworth. "When I came in '77, that was the only place for dim sum. And then dim sum caught on. Started out it was just served on Sundays. And then it was Sundays and Saturdays. And it was only around noon time." At traditional Chinatown dim sum houses such as Phoenix, MingHin, and Cai, customers can pick and choose their selections right off the pushcarts that roam the restaurant. At Won Kow, customers order dim sum from a large laminated menu, guided by vivid color photos of each dish. Popular choices are the BBQ pork *bao*, the steamed pork dumplings, and the shrimp and cilantro dumplings. They arrive at the table fresh and hot in metal steamers. The wrappers are mostly made with rice flour and water. "You can think of it as Chinese tapas," says Rohsenow.

An entire side of Won Kow's large kitchen is devoted to dim sum. Stacks of steamers and baskets are piled high. Each dim sum dish is made from scratch, with staff meticulously forming row after row of perfectly shaped pot stickers and dumplings. During meal service, a din rises from the steamers and crackling woks firing on all cylinders, mixed with high-spirited chatter among the staff, some who have been with Won Kow for fifteen years or more.

Won Kow started serving dim sum in 1990, when Peter and his brother took over the restaurant. "Maybe a little earlier," says Peter, who struggles with exact dates even though his memory is clearly sharp. Its popularity has declined "gradually": Peter used to open at 9:00 A.M. daily for dim sum service. Now, he opens at 10:30 A.M., as the dim sum business on the old-guard side of town has been "less and less." The restaurant used to be open well past midnight to accommodate a late-night crowd, but over the years, Peter gradually inched toward an 11 P.M. closing time, shortening the number of work shifts to just two.

I pondered Won Kow's waning business one morning while feasting on delicate dumplings made fresh just moments beforehand. Peter worries about staying relevant in a neighborhood where the Cantonese culture is slowly but surely disappearing. He shouldn't have to worry, I thought, as I gobbled up the mouthwatering barbecued pork *bao* that cost just a few bucks per order. If anything, Won Kow should be more popular than ever, considering the current focus on fresh ingredients and slow-cooked cuisine. I silently wished a renaissance upon this fading institution as I took a stab at a rice crepe, so silky it slipped out of my chopsticks.

Cantonese versus Mandarin, Huey versus Hoy

In 1949, the Chinese Communist Party established the People's Republic of China (PRC) on the mainland, while the Republic of China retreated with Chiang Kai-shek to the island of Taiwan. This pivotal moment sparked enormous conflicts, prompting scores of families to seek refuge for religious, political, and economic reasons. Many Cantonese-speaking immigrants and refugees from China and Hong Kong who subsequently arrived in Chicago initially settled around Chinatown, joining the second-generation community in renovating and expanding what some now call "South Side Chinatown" or "Old Chinatown" (Rohsenow 2003).

When he left Hong Kong in 1950, Peter says, no one spoke Mandarin —in his native village or his new city of Chicago. Cantonese has been the native dialect for the vast majority of foreign-born Chinatown residents like Peter. In 1975, some estimated that as many as 90 percent of Chinatown's residents spoke Cantonese or Toishan (Lau 2006, 177). With Mandarin Chinese considered the official dialect of both the PRC and Taiwan, however, Cantonese is being slowly phased out. "Even now, in the south part of China and Hong Kong, they speak Mandarin," explained Peter, "but not exactly 100 percent."

Somewhere around 2005, Peter started to hear more Mandarin in the neighborhood. This reflects a more diverse Chinese community in Chicago, as immigration from China has become increasingly easier. Chinese immigrate to Chicago from all over China, not just Canton, and Chinatown is now more multicultural as a result. To this day, however, Won Kow's staff speak only Cantonese and some English. Peter hires Cantonese-speaking staff to accommodate the regulars who phone in takeout orders. Staff are "mostly from Hong Kong," explains Peter. "We can speak the village dialect. Everybody knows everybody."

Won Kow
staff member

Chinese Takeout Containers: A Chicago Invention

The Chinese takeout container has been around since the late 1800s. I've seen this iconic design stomping down the runway for a high-end handbag line. I've also witnessed a takeout container costume on a man parading down Halsted Street on Halloween night. But mostly I've wrestled Chinese takeout with my chopsticks from these little white boxes on nights when I found myself too tired to cook or simply craved the sesame chicken from Yen's on Clark Street. The design belongs to Frederick Weeks Wilcox, a Chicago inventor who was granted the patent on November 13, 1894.

Wilcox's patent was for a "food pail" consisting of one piece of paper and a wire handle. Originally used to transport oysters, the food pail's origami-influenced design is simple but genius: one piece of folding paperboard coated with polyethylene to make it leakproof, topped with a single wire handle. The innovative pail prevents liquids from leaking out and keeps cold food cold and hot food hot, letting steam escape through the top folds.

Bloomer Brothers started manufacturing these food pails sometime around 1900, adding the signature red pagoda and "Thank You" graphics around 1970. Bloomer Brothers was renamed Fold-Pak in 1977. Now headquartered in Georgia, Fold-Pak is the largest takeout container manufacturer in the world, producing 300 million Chinese takeout containers per year. Today the company produces several different kinds of takeout containers, uses recyclable and environmentally friendly materials, and offers microwave-safe handles.

Their most popular item? The plain white Chinese takeout container in pint and quart sizes, says Director of Corporate Communications Chris Augustine. No patents are left on the box, Augustine says.

Chop suey in a Chinese takeout container. Now that's American.

Peter's family name—Hoy—was altered to Huey by the nuns who taught him back in Canton. His wife, children, and grandchildren all use Huey, but his brother's family, who stayed in Toisan, use the original spelling of Hoy. (The Won Kow business card shows two different last names: Peter Huey and David Hoy.) "Huey, see, it's a little different," explained Peter one morning. "Once you have it, you usually keep it. I can change it. But, no sense changing back and forth."

Chinese-American children are now being taught English and Mandarin in Chicago's schools, creating a giant cultural divide in families whose older generations speak Cantonese. Language isn't the only generational barrier. The second generation of Chinese Americans took over family restaurants in Chinatown, but not the third, says Kenny Chiu, manager and co-owner at Emperor's Choice at 2238 South Wentworth. Almost all of the old restaurants are gone, he says. The children don't want to take over. They "have no interest in it," he says from his usual station front of house. "Restaurant life is hard."

Chiu came to Chinatown in 1980. He started working at Emperor's Choice as a server in 1993, when it was owned by Ronald Moy, from the same Moy family that originally owned Won Kow. "The old museum was in a grocery store," he remembers, referring to the Chinese American Museum of Chicago now on West Twenty-Third Street. Emperor's Choice is one of the few old-guard restaurants that continues to flourish. Chiu and his business partners remodeled the space in 2013 with modern finishes and a sleek bar. One can still get a glimpse of old-guard elements, like the set of imperial robes from China's Qing dynasty hanging on the wall, or the sight of staff hand-shelling mountains of water chestnuts and snap peas at a back table.

When Peter's brother and sister-in-law passed away, they handed down their half of the corporation, which owns Won Kow's building, to their sons, David, Ronald, and Robert. David manages the night shift at Won Kow. Robert runs Hoypoloi Gallery on the ground floor, while Ronald is a practicing attorney. Peter also has three children. They all work in other lines of business, are pursuing advanced degrees, or both. Peter is reluctant to discuss his children when it comes to taking over Won Kow. He offered that his children and his wife, who is thirty years his junior, help out at the restaurant during busy times such as Chinese New Year. Other than David and a family cousin, however, no other family members seem to work regularly at the restaurant.

"I still thinking about selling it," Peter says of his building. Now he may actually find a buyer. "Somebody want to buy it now. Because people from China, they have so much money. They are looking for businesses" in which to invest. Rohsenow has seen this new interest at the Chinese American Museum, as well. "Since the '80s and '90s, the mainland Chinese are getting a much better deal. They've got more money to throw around. They come around every year, at Chinese New Year, and they give us money in a red envelope. This is the pressure of doing business in China."

Chinese investors are pouring money into Chicago, sensing affordable real estate development opportunities. According to a report by the Asia Society and Rosen Consulting, Chinese investors purchased more than $93 billion of residential real estate and $17.1 billion of commercial real estate in the United States between 2005 and 2015—the highest of any foreign group. The growth is partly fueled by the EB-5 visa program, which grants immigration visas to foreigners investing at least a half-million dollars in real estate development (Eldredge 2016). Interest in Chicago's Chinatown is also fueled by significant population surges in the area. According to the U.S. Census, Chicago's Chinese population grew by more than 50 percent from 2000 to 2014. Many are settling in Chinatown's bordering neighborhoods of Armour Square and Bridgeport.

After trying unsuccessfully to sell his building since 1970, Peter finally may find himself in the enviable position of juggling offers in the modern-day grab for Chinatown's real estate. "If I give it up, I don't know what to do," he says of his long-time business, but he admits that "even though I take it easy a little bit better . . . I'm too old [to be] running around."

While Peter and I talked at Won Kow one day, a string of hits from Madonna, Joan Jett, and Cyndi Lauper played overhead from the restaurant's sound system. A large group of school kids, most likely on a field trip, swarmed in for lunch and took over several of the large tables near the windows, spinning the lazy Susans to life.

"I'm just back and forth," Peter says about selling the building he has poured more than half his life into. "I figure, I give it up, what am I gonna do with myself? I might as well keep it for a while and see how it is. That's how I feel now."

When Peter Huey and his brother Robert purchased Won Kow in 1970, they found several tiki cocktail recipes behind the bar, all handwritten on index cards. They were apparently left behind by the original owners, the Moys. These cocktails can be ordered individually or "flaming volcano" style for groups. Flaming volcano drinks are served in colorful ceramic bowls and are sipped communally from large straws. The server places a cup of booze in the middle and sets it aflame. Freshly squeezed juice works best for these cocktails.

Zombie

Ingredients

1 oz. dark Jamaican rum
½ oz. light rum
½ oz. orange curacao
½ oz. sweet vermouth
½ oz. lemon juice
1 oz. orange juice
1 oz. pineapple juice

Directions

1. Fill mixing glass with ice.
2. Add all ingredients, shake.
3. Strain into a Collins glass filled with ice.
4. Garnish with a cherry.

Scorpion

Ingredients

2 oz. light rum
1 oz. brandy
2 oz. orange juice
½ oz. lemon juice
½ oz. cream de noyaux (almond)

Directions

1. Fill blender with 3 oz. crushed ice and the light rum, brandy, orange juice, lemon juice and cream de noyaux (almond).
2. Blend until smooth.
3. Pour into a highball glass.
4. Garnish with a slice of orange.

Two

TUFANO'S VERNON PARK TAP
A Long Lifeline in Little Italy

Tufano's Vernon Park Tap, opened in 1930 by Theresa Tufano DiBuono and Joseph DiBuono, is nearly impossible to find. It's located in Little Italy at 1073 West Vernon Park Place, a street that runs for only a few blocks: Racine to Morgan, and Des Plaines to Clinton. The only way to drive directly to Tufano's is to turn east onto Vernon Park Place from Racine, as through streets from the east, south, and north are blocked off by cul-de-sacs and a parking lot for the University of Illinois Chicago (UIC). Tufano's does not have a sign. It does little, if any, advertising. Yet every night, the 180-seat restaurant and bar are packed with multiple generations of regulars, local sports figures, and tourists looking for an Old World Italian place in Chicago.

When a family restaurant has been in business for four generations, I want to know their secret. Not their secret sauce, necessarily, but the glue that has held this family together for decades. Is it a matriarch or patriarch? How has Tufano's somehow managed to sidestep the differences that destroy other family businesses? Differences such as language and culture. Age-old arguments that never get settled.

Legal and financial woes. Divorce. What does this place have that other family businesses don't?

It doesn't come down to one ingredient. But if you ask anyone today what holds Tufano's together, they'll say it's Joey DiBuono, who's worked at the restaurant since he was a teenager busing tables and making salads, taking over in the 1980s as a third-generation owner and operator. And if you ask Joey why Tufano's has been successful since 1930, he starts naming family members as though giving an acceptance speech at an award ceremony. Many have since passed but worked tirelessly at the restaurant before, one by one, they handed him the reins.

He names his father, Salvatore, whom he calls his mentor. And his grandmother Theresa, who toiled in the restaurant's kitchen for sixty-five years. His mother, Marie, who cooked every morning alongside her mother and let Joey build a back dining room where her garage used to be. His great-aunt Toni, who gave him the lot next door so that he could build what is now the main dining room.

Aunt Rose, his father's sister, who also cooked every day in the restaurant's original tiny kitchen with the rest of the family. Sisters Teresa and Joann, who dove in and helped when their ancestors got older and experienced health problems. Another aunt, Anna Marie, who thinks of Joey as her son. His wife, Tracy, who he's been married to since 1982. His daughter Darci, the day manager and catering and special events coordinator . . .

"I've had a great support system over the years," Joey says on a quiet Monday, the one day a week when the restaurant is closed. "A lot of people say, you're lucky, you're third generation, nobody does this anymore. I wanna do it. And my daughter wants to. I'm very happy and content with what we have here. And I'm fortunate. We're blessed and we're lucky."

Tufano's Bakery: "The Best Pizza in the City of Chicago"

Before there was Tufano's Vernon Park Tap, there was Tufano's Bakery down the street at 628 South Aberdeen. It was demolished in the '60s with the rest of the block for a University of Illinois parking lot. Joey's great-grandparents Marie and Dominic Tufano opened the bakery when they first came to Chicago from Acerra, Italy, in the early twentieth century, an era that brought tens of thousands of Italian immigrants to Chicago (Candeloro 1995, 230).

Anna Marie DiBuono is Marie and Dominic's granddaughter and Theresa and Joseph DiBuono's youngest child. She is the last surviving member of her generation. "My father was Al Capone's chef," says Anna Marie. "So you know my father was a good chef!" she says, laughing. "That's what my mother always said: 'Your father is better than I am!'"

When she was born in 1938, her family lived on South Aberdeen next to the bakery. "My grandfather came from Naples originally, before my grandmother and my mother," says Anna Marie, who still lives in the building next to Tufano's Vernon Park Tap, where her family moved in 1944. "My grandpa must have come around 1904, and my mother and my grandmother, I think, in 1907. My mother was six." Many Italians who settled on Vernon Park Place and the surrounding streets also came from Acerra, a town within Naples. "Most of the people in this section right here all came from the same town. So we all knew each other."

Theresa Tufano DiBuono and Joseph DiBuono

Tufano's Bakery made Neapolitan pizza and breads from about 1910 until it closed in the late 1940s. During the Depression, customers would make their own bread at home, carve their initials in the dough, and bring it to the bakery, where Marie would bake it in the oven for a penny. Theresa eventually took over for her mother, baking fresh breads and square-cut pizzas for the neighborhood, which people referred to as Taylor Street, even if they didn't live on Taylor itself. The neighborhood's moniker of Little Italy came later, Anna Marie says. And they never call it by its most recent label: University Village. "We're Taylor Street. There's Grand Avenue (where many Italian immigrants also settled), and we're Taylor Street."

Pepe Osicco

When Tufano's Vernon Park Tap first opened, locals referred to it as Pepe Osicco's—Joseph DiBuono's nickname. It was a bar with a few tables in front, a dozen tables in back, and a small kitchen in the middle. People in the neighborhood started bringing pizza from Tufano's Bakery over to the bar, which did not serve food at first. "It operated more as a tavern in those days," recalls Anna Marie, whose resemblance to her mother is evident in a photo that hangs in the restaurant. "They'd cover the pizza and bring it into the restaurant. Then my father added on a room back here," she says, pointing to the back of her apartment, "and we had a pizza oven there. It was a brick oven. Gas heat. The guy came from New York, he built it right in the house, in this apartment, at 1071 West Vernon Park. Friday, Saturday, and Sunday my mother made pizza. And we had a window. We used to pass the pizza through the little window into the restaurant."

Anna Marie looks off into the distance remembering her mother's pizza. "She used San Marzano tomatoes, the real mozzarella, not the stuff they use today, we used to braid it ourselves. Basil and stuff. It was just not to be believed. She used to use Ceresota flour and dry yeast that she'd mix with the water and salt . . . She made the best pizza in the city of Chicago. God rest her soul."

After Tufano's Bakery closed in the late 1940s, Theresa continued to make her prized pizza in the brick oven, sliding it through the pass-through window to Tufano's Vernon Park Tap. Tufano's pizza

Tufano's chalkboard

brings fond memories to those lucky enough to indulge. "The older kids in the neighborhood will always say, 'Oh God, Tufano's had the best pizza!'" Anna Marie says.

"They used to make the best pizza," echoes Joey. "My grandmother, her mother, never got any recognition for it. It was phenomenal. Very thin and light. People still talk about the pizza."

Theresa stopped making pizza in the late '70s, and the brick oven was dismantled a few years later. "My grandma . . . she said she didn't want the oven anymore. It just got to be too much. It's the one thing I regret getting rid of," Joey says. Tufano's staff will proudly point out the pass-through window, still visible from the kitchen. The other side was sealed off in what is now Anna Marie's bedroom. "I asked them to seal it off. Otherwise it would smell like calamari in here."

Other remnants of Tufano's past also remain, including the top of the original bar, Joseph DiBuono's clock, and the cash-only policy—almost unheard of in the city of Chicago. "If people are stuck, they'll send me a check," Joey says with a shrug. "They can't believe it. It's happened lots of times. And people will say to this day, 'You said I could send you a check, that was so nice of you.' Never got stiffed."

After World War II ended, the second generation of the Tufano and DiBuono families joined the business, including Joey's parents, Marie and Salvatore, or Sammy D.A., as his friends called him. Everyone cooked at some point. "My father greeted everybody and worked behind the bar, and he also cooked a little bit," Joey says of his father, who passed away in 1983. "My mother cooked every morning with my grandmother. Aunt Rose also came in every morning and helped. That was my father's sister. And the other person who was instrumental was my Aunt Toni, my grandmother's sister, who lived next door. She was very supportive of me."

Antoinette, or Toni, Tufano made her famous raviolis for Tufano's up until just a few years before she passed away in 2014 at the age of ninety-nine. "She made raviolis like you couldn't believe," says Anna Marie of her aunt. "My sister, my aunt, my mother . . . They worked together. They really complemented each other. I waited on

From left: *Anne Marie DiBuono, Theresa Tufano DiBuono, Marie Tufano, Rose DiBuono Alesia, and Antoinette Tufano at Salvatore and Marie DiBuono's wedding in 1948 at the Shrine of Our Lady of Pompeii*

tables in the old days and stuff. It was so much fun. It was more like a club than a restaurant. Everybody knew each other. Everybody was so friendly and close. Even today it's still like that."

UIC Changed Little Italy's History

In the 1960s, about one square mile of the Little Italy neighborhood was demolished to make way for the University of Illinois Chicago branch (Candeloro 1995, 244). It was called the Chicago Circle campus until 1982, when it merged with the university's medical campus to form UIC. Miraculously, Tufano's Vernon Park Tap was spared. "We were on the right side of the street when the university was built," Joey says of his address on the south side of Vernon Park. "Thank God we weren't on the other side."

The immediate area wasn't so lucky. A network of Italian-owned grocery stores and taverns on Vernon Park, Aberdeen, Carpenter, and other streets in the area all got torn down when the university arrived. Aberdeen, Carpenter, and May all became cul-de-sacs at Vernon Park Place. The city cemented over the lot next to Tufano's, where the neighborhood kids once played street hockey and baseball. "It changed the whole history of the neighborhood," says Joey. "I always said, if the university never came, we'd be like the North End of Boston. Back in those days, people came here and started a little business, whether it be a bakery or a restaurant, grocery store, that's what they did for a living. Times have changed."

The university requested that Tufano's take their beer sign down for reasons the family isn't quite clear on. "It didn't say Tufano's. It just had Hamm's" on it, says Anna Marie. "There was never a sign with Tufano's on it. It was just a beer sign." When the university told Tufano's they were allowed to place the sign back up, the family didn't bother. It seems operating without any sign for more than half a century works just fine.

From 50 to 180 Seats in 10 Years

Growing up surrounded by two older generations, Joey had a rare, front-row seat to running a Southern Italian restaurant the Old World way. "I was blessed to be in here when I was young," he says. "I was in here every day. I saw how my dad treated people. My dad was instrumental in showing me how to treat people. It never cost anything to be nice to people. Be respectful, always look somebody in the eye, and be nice. I was fortunate that my dad taught me that. I taught that to my daughters."

Joey DiBuono

Joey was poised for a hockey scholarship at Loyola University, but a career in sports was cut short by a head injury. "That kind of ended my hockey career. I never went to Loyola. There's always a reason things happen. I don't regret it." After his father, Salvatore, lost a battle with cancer in 1983, Joey poured himself into the restaurant. "Joey just took over," Anna Marie affirms. "And it grew."

For more than fifty years, the family worked elbow to elbow in Tufano's tiny kitchen, as customers endured long waits for food or one of the coveted seats. They used what is now Anna Marie's bedroom as an auxiliary kitchen, sliding plates through the pass-through window.

Joey knew the restaurant could no longer function with its limited capacity. "First of all, the equipment was obsolete," he says. "I told my grandmother, we can't keep working like this. It's just too hard. I used to have to ask people, 'Can you please get up?' when they were waiting, and I hated doing that. I mean, it got crazy. People waited a long time. The kitchen was really small."

In 1987, Joey's great-aunt Toni gave him the lot next door to Tufano's, and he added what is now the main dining room. He used the front of the building as a garden until the city approved plans to build out additional space, adding the front dining room in 1989, the same year he broke ground in the backyard to expand the kitchen with additional prep space, a walk-in cooler, and a kettle for the gravy. The Tufanos and DiBuonos don't call it tomato sauce. They call it gravy. "Even in New York, New Jersey, they call it gravy," says Anna Marie. Tufano's gravy is a tomato sauce cooked in meat that is strained out before it's served. Their marinara is made just with tomatoes—no meat. Anna Marie's generation also uses the term macaroni, not pasta. "No matter what we were eating, we were eating macaroni," she says. "We never called it pasta. We always called it macaroni."

Some of the dishes scrawled out on the restaurant's chalkboards have flourished on the menu since it was Pepe Osicco's place. Lemon chicken is one of them. Before Joey upgraded the cramped kitchen, customers were forced to wait for this Tufano's specialty, which requires long cooking times under a hot broiler. "The first piece of commercial kitchen equipment I bought was this broiler, especially to cook the lemon chicken," Joey says, proudly pointing to the huge broiler that churns out an average of thirty orders a day.

The mid 1990s brought a flood of new customers seeking a meal before a Bulls or Blackhawks game at the United Center, which opened in 1994 on Madison, less than two miles from the restaurant. Joey refers to this era as "the Jordan days." So he added the back dining room, which was originally his mother's garage. "I said, 'Mom, I got an idea.' She said, 'What's that, Joey?' I said, 'Well, you know, we're like crazy busy, I was thinking of putting the room there.' My mother used to swear at me all the time. That's how my mother was. She said, 'Are you #@$%&*! crazy?' I said, 'No.' She said, 'OK, if that's what you wanna do.' So we added that room on. We use it for bigger

31

parties and rehearsal dinners and stuff like that. We still call it the new room."

Tufano's went from a humble space seating 50 into a full-service, 180-seat restaurant and bar in only about 10 years' time under Joey's watch. "It's just phenomenal how a little bakery, and then a little place, grew into what Tufano's is today, thanks to Joey," says Anna Marie of her nephew. Sometime around 2005, Tufano's acquired a patio license from the city and added outdoor seating—a peaceful, idyllic spot next to a gurgling fountain that the city installed around the same time. Diners can now enjoy a romantic meal al fresco where the neighborhoods kids used to play spirited games of baseball and street hockey.

Tufano's Then and Now
Chalkboards and Computers

Like everything else at Tufano's, the menu is a combination of old and new traditions. Standbys include the lemon chicken, eggplant parmigiana, meatballs, pork chops and peppers, and tripe. "I'm one of the few Italian restaurants that serves tripe," says Joey. "I get people calling me all the time saying, 'Joey you got any tripe?' That's my grandmother's recipe. It's very old world, and people still like it." In the '50s and '60s, folks in the neighborhood would bring pans to Tufano's and fill them up with tripe or, on Fridays and during Lent, pans of pasta *fagioli*. Tufano's also served lung stew. "That was a big seller," says Anna Marie. "They also used to do broiled sweetbreads. That was before everybody changed their diets." Tufano's used to offer eggplant parmigiana only on Tuesdays, Wednesdays, and Thursdays, but the kitchen ran out daily, so "eggplant parm" made it to the regular menu around 2005. "It's lighter," Joey explains when asked what makes his version so popular. "There's no breading at all. No breadcrumbs. Just flour and egg."

Tufano's sources its olive oil and certain varieties of cheese from Italy, but most ingredients are now available locally—their bread is from Turano in Berwyn—or through one of the city's many distributors like Greco & Sons. "The key, to me, is having consistent food, no matter what," Joey says when asked what has kept Tufano's doors open for almost ninety years. "You have to watch what you buy. I don't go the cheap route. And another thing is price point. I think our price point is very good."

New menu items, which, in Tufano's case, means dishes added within the last fifty years, have gradually appeared over time. They include chicken picante with *pinoli*, Tufano's special salad, shells and broccoli, ravioli with meat, gluten-free pasta—available on request—Bolognese sauce, grilled calamari, and pasta with vodka sauce and peas, or the "D&D special," a dish inspired by Joey's twin daughters, Darci and Disa. At one point, both sisters were serving tables at the restaurant. "You know, at the end of your shift, you're hungry," says Darci, who became Darci Pinello in 2015, when she was married at The Shrine of Our Lady of Pompeii, the same church where her grandparents and great-grandparents were married and the oldest Italian-American church in continuous use in Chicago (Catrambone and Shubart 2007, 112). "My sister would always get shells with vodka sauce. She would eat it, then I'd finish hers, and I'd have to go get more, and I'd get it with peas. And then we'd both finish it together. I said, 'We should put this on the menu.' That's how it started."

Darci started working at Tufano's at the same age as her father—sixteen. She immediately fell in love with the adrenaline of executing a lunch or dinner shift. Disa, who in 2016 was also married at The Shrine of Our Lady of Pompeii, didn't feel the same pull of restaurant life, and she switched to a career in law after about a year of working at her family's restaurant. Darci became the restaurant's manager in 2011 after earning a degree in communications from DePaul University. She now coordinates catering services and books parties and special events. "I started waitressing when I was eighteen, and I *loved* it. Now that I have a baby I don't waitress as much. But if I need to get on the floor, I can do it [*snaps her fingers*]—no problem. And I love it! Just the adrenaline rush of executing it all."

Darci and her father both have the same humble, easygoing, gracious personality. They routinely bounce ideas off each other, maintaining a symbiotic work relationship. "I'm very lucky that my dad's not stuck in his ways," says Darci, a striking brunette who lives in the northern suburbs but maintains an apartment above the family's restaurant, where she brings her daughter, Sophia, a couple of days a week. "He's very open. I'm very grateful for that. I think that's why we are still here, because he's open, he's always looking to make it the best it can be here." Darci built a desperately needed website for Tufano's in 2011 and brought in a new touchscreen ordering system in 2014, after the outdated system crashed on a night with a full house, forcing staff to dash off handwritten orders and tally checks manually.

Darci's penmanship has come in handy with the restaurant's menu, which is handwritten on chalkboards all over the restaurant. "People were complaining they could not read the boards," says Darci, whose request to replace the old chalkboards—original to the restaurant—was denied. "That's when the whole chalkboard paint became really popular for kids. So on my day off, on Monday, when the restaurant's completely closed, I came here by myself, got on a ladder, and I wiped down all the boards and I repainted them. I was here for like twelve hours alone on a Monday. And then Tuesday, before we opened, I got back on the ladder and rewrote the boards. And it was legible."

Word-of-Mouth to Foodie Apps

You'll learn more about Tufano's from the framed clippings on the wall than a quick search on Google. Joey hasn't invested much in his restaurant's online reputation—something businesses spend enormous amounts of time and money to manage. "Maybe I ignore it, maybe I shouldn't," he says of responding to reviews customers leave on Yelp, Facebook, and other consumer-generated sites.

Defying expectations of her generation, Darci agrees, not giving much credence to online reviews, either personally or professionally. "The way my dad raised me, and the way I am, is that if you have nothing nice to say, don't say anything at all. And listen, even if you go to the best restaurant, something might not be perfect. But I'm not gonna knock them. Everyone's trying. You come here, we're all trying to give you the best service. There are always going to be bumps along the way. That's life." Tufano's serves anywhere from 150 to 300 customers a day, six days a week, fifty-two weeks a year. "Realistically, that's a lot of people to try to please, and it's hard to do that. So we try to be kind and nice. While they're here, if something comes up, we'll act on it immediately and try to help. Even when I go and try new restaurants, I don't go on Yelp to see what the ratings are. Maybe I'm old school, but I just don't." By her father's estimation, people leave the restaurant happy 95 percent of the time. Yelp schmelp.

Word-of-mouth advertising has always worked for Tufano's, which is essential for a restaurant with a hard-to-find location on a dead-end street. A couple blocks south, restaurants can rely on the pedestrian traffic from Taylor Street, Little Italy's commercial strip. Tufano's doesn't find you, you find Tufano's. "We're on a residential side street, so you have to find your way to us," says Darci, who estimates that word of mouth accounts for about 90 percent of their business. "We don't work with hotel concierges. We're not that type of restaurant." But a feature on the Food Network's *Diners, Drive-Ins, and Dives* in 2008 brought a huge wave of new customers from all over the United States and Canada—and continues to bring in business whenever the episode repeats. "That made us a destination spot for people coming to Chicago that we would not normally touch base with," says Darci. "They can come right to us from the app. We've always watched the show, but we didn't know the magnitude of what it really could do."

Joey credits the show for bringing in more new business than any other media mention or culinary award, which includes a James Beard Foundation America's Classics Award in 2008 (the Berghoff and Calumet Fisheries are two other Chicago recipients). "It's remarkable the following he has," Joey says of the show's host, Guy Fieri. "People look him up, they see I got a good review, and they'll tell me they saw it on *Diners, Drive-Ins, and Dives*. I've never seen a following like that."

Italian Singers to Sports Figures

Celebrity sightings are common at Tufano's. In the '40s, '50s and '60s, Nelson Algren, Frank Sinatra, Tony Bennett, Jerry Vale, the Maguire sisters, and Jerry Lewis stopped in for a plate of eggplant parmigiana or pork chops and peppers. "The two celebrities that customers really went crazy for were Federico Castelluccio [Furio Fiunta on *The Sopranos*] and Jack Nicholson. That was crazy. Jack was here twice. I'll never forget that, when he came back the second time. The Hawks were in the finals."

Starting in the '80s, sports figures like Bobby Hull were frequently found at Tufano's, drawn by the restaurant's proximity to the United Center. "By that time, the Italian singers were old," says Anna Marie. Framed Blackhawks jerseys and other sports memorabilia now festoon Tufano's walls, and customers watch Bulls and Blackhawks games from the bar or "the new room" in back.

Taylor Street to University Village

Just as Tufano's has many names—Pepe Osicco's, Tufano's Vernon Park Tap, Vernon Park Tap, or just Tufano's—the surrounding neighborhood also has seen a succession of names throughout its history, from Taylor Street, to Little Italy, to Tri-Taylor, and, more recently, University Village.

As an Italian-American kid growing up in Chicago, Joey was asked whether he was from Taylor Street, Bridgeport, Chinatown, Grand Avenue, or Chicago Avenue—all areas that have (or had) a strong Italian identity. Joey always answered Taylor Street. "That's how I consider myself, where I came from. The Tufanos have a good lifeline. We've lived here all our lives."

Four generations of the family have lived either in the apartments above Tufano's or in the buildings next door. Disa moved into the same house Joey grew up in, two doors down from the restaurant. Anna Marie has lived in the same building next door since 1944, where the family cooked up a storm in what served as the restaurant's auxiliary kitchen from the '30s to the '80s. The Tufanos and DiBuonos aren't the only families who have lived on the same block in Little Italy their entire lives. "There are still a lot of people that live around here in the neighborhood," maintained Joey. "A lot of people that grew up here."

The area is also called the Near West Side or Area 28, a region that was radically reshaped in the second half of the twentieth century by new expressways and UIC. These developments wiped out not only a significant portion of Little Italy, razing two-thirds of the housing in the Our Lady of Pompeii parish (Catrambone and Shubart 2007, 99), but also Chicago's first Greektown, which was bounded by Harrison, Polk, Halsted, and Blue Island. Developments also wiped out Hull

House, the influential settlement house established by Jane Addams and Ellen Gates Starr in 1889.

The Near West Side evokes a reputation for violent crime, a low-income population, and racial tensions. But walk around the immediate area surrounding Tufano's, an intricate network of one-way streets and cul-de-sacs on either side of Racine, and you'll come across streets like Lexington. Fluorney. Vernon Park Place. Streets that are sheltered from the strife of other parts of the Near West Side. Well-kept two-flats and apartment buildings that swell with pride. Old, historic red brick structures that show signs of age yet decades of care. The Shrine of Our Lady of Pompeii on Lexington and Notre Dame de Chicago on Harrison, two Catholic parishes founded more than a century ago, soar over the neighborhood. Arrigo and Sheridan parks invite locals for a game of baseball or leisurely stroll under the shade of old trees. Even with UIC taking over some of the housing, the peaceful neighborhood is in sharp contrast to the chaos and cacophony of screaming ambulances and roaring expressways just a couple of blocks away.

Tufano's Offspring and Long-Time Staff

Foodies around the country have likely heard of Blackbird, Chicago's critically acclaimed restaurant on Randolph Street. Before owner Donny Madia opened this sleek, elegant eatery, he tended bar at Tufano's. His friendship with Joey goes back to Gordon Tech High School, now known as DePaul College Prep. "Donny holds a special place in my heart," says Joey. "He's a really special friend. He had a vision, and he worked really hard at his vision. I'm very proud of him." Along with Blackbird, Madia also executed his vision at avec, Publican, Violet Hour, Big Star, and Nico Osteria in Chicago.

Tarantino's is another restaurant owned by a Tufano's alum. This elegant Italian eatery in Lincoln Park is owned by Johnny "JT" Tarantino, Joey's wife's cousin, who served tables at Tufano's for a long time. Joey DeVito also passed through Tufano's doors before opening the nationally known Busy Burger on Taylor Street; Paul Heatherington, who helms Ats a Nice Pizza (a name that only works if you say it with your hands) in Romeoville, Illinois, is yet another.

Other staff members boast long tenures at Tufano's, staying for ten, twenty, even thirty years and longer. Tony Di Vittorio was chef from the early 1980s until he passed away in 2013. Some of the servers who masterfully blaze through a busy lunch or dinner shift have clocked in decades apiece. Bobbie Spizzinoco, or "Bobbie Red," has worked for the family since 1983, fellow server Judy DeMarie since 1986. Joey's sisters Joann and Teresa have also been fixtures on and off throughout the restaurant's history. "I make sure I have the right people working for me, which is very key," Joey says. "You treat people well, they're gonna respect you and do a good job for you."

"I'm usually here," he continues. "If I'm not here, my sisters are here or my daughter is here. I know people by name which is, to me, very important. You know people. You know what they're going to eat. I see kids from the neighborhood coming in with dates, they're having

their wedding rehearsal dinner here now. To me, that's an honor to have that for them, to keep coming back here for their birthdays or anything. And it's really nice that I've been able to do it. People say, why don't you have another restaurant? I've gotten that question a million times, and I've had opportunities . . . First of all, life's too short, and this is hard enough as it

is. I've been blessed to have this restaurant . . . to continue the tradition of making people feel good, enjoying food, just sitting down and having a little glass of wine just chilling out. It's important to sit around and enjoy your friends and have a bowl of pasta or some chicken and have a good time. Everybody's just so caught up in the world of craziness. One guy, recently he was sick, and his wife said, Joey, the first thing he said when he woke up was 'I want Tufano's chicken.' I started crying. How touching is that? It's just a nice feeling. That you know you're making people feel good."

A meal at Tufano's can be an emotional experience. Time feels frozen on Vernon Park Place. Memories seem baked into the street, where folks once walked Marie Tufano's pizza over to Pepe Osicco's. The traditions of Italian families who have worshipped, lived, and celebrated here have somehow been preserved since 1930. Anna Marie says it best: "Times change, nothing stays the same. Except Tufano's."

In 1930, the same year Tufano's Vernon Park Tap opened:

- William "Big Bill" Thompson was mayor of Chicago
- Chicago's population was 3.4 million
- Chicago was at the height of economic expansion
- The Merchandise Mart opened, becoming the world's largest building
- The Twinkie was invented by James Dewar at Continental Baking Company in Schiller Park
- A gallon of gas was ten cents
- Bill Veeck was president of the Chicago Cubs
- The Chicago White Sox finished seventh in the American League

Tufano's Fried Calamari

Tufano's started offering this dish in 1987, after Joey DiBuono was able to expand the dining room and kitchen, where he added a deep fryer to the line. This is one of Joey's recipes; he uses milk to make the calamari more tender. (The amount of oil indicated is for use with a deep fryer.)

Ingredients
1 bottle of vegetable oil
2 lb. cut calamari
6 whole eggs
1½ c. milk
1 t. salt
½ t. pepper
4 c. flour

Directions

1. Set a deep fryer to 450°. Fill the deep fryer with vegetable oil. Start with 1 bottle; add more later, as needed.

2. Rinse the calamari, placing in a strainer to drain out water.

3. In a separate bowl, make a wash, using the eggs, milk, salt, and pepper. With a whisk, beat all the ingredients for about a minute or until fully combined.

4. Add the rinsed calamari to the bowl with the egg mixture. Let it soak for a few minutes.

5. Place flour in a separate bowl. Start out with 4 cups of flour; add more as needed.

6. Scoop out 2 cups of the drained calamari—a strainer works best—and place calamari in the bowl of flour. Toss calamari gently in flour, making sure each piece is evenly coated with flour.

7. Take your coated calamari and place it into another, dry strainer. Shake off excess flour.

8. Before putting coated calamari into the deep fryer, make sure it is hot and ready. We recommend that you test one piece of calamari to make sure the oil is hot enough.

9. Fry the calamari in small batches. Take it out when golden and drain it on paper towels.

10. Plate the calamari and serve with fresh lemons and marinara sauce.

Tufano's Lemon Chicken

This is one of Theresa Tufano DiBuono and Joseph DiBuono's signature recipes, which Tufano's has served since 1930. Nearly ninety years later, it is still one of their most requested menu items. The recipe calls for one lemon, but I prefer using two—one juiced and one sliced. A simple yet extremely delicious dish.

Ingredients

1 whole chicken	4 cloves minced garlic
½ tsp. salt	¼ cup olive oil
½ tsp. pepper	¼ cup vegetable oil
1 tsp. dried oregano	1 lemon

Directions

1. Preheat broiler to highest level of heat.
2. Rinse the chicken and pat dry. Cut chicken into pieces, yielding 2 ¾ lb.
3. Place the pieces of chicken into a broiler pan. Make sure the pieces lay flat in the pan.
4. Season chicken with the salt, pepper, oregano, and garlic. Drizzle chicken with the olive oil and vegetable oil.
5. Cut the lemon in half and squeeze the fresh juice over the chicken. After that, place the lemon pieces in the pan with the chicken.
6. Place your pan in the broiler. Cook the chicken on one side for about 20–25 minutes, then turn over and cook the other side until chicken is golden and crispy. *Do not* overcook chicken. Turning ensures that the chicken gets even coloring and does not burn on one side.
7. Once chicken is fully cooked, remove from broiler and plate with cottage fried potatoes.
8. To finish the dish, pour the pan juice over the chicken and potatoes and serve.

Three

THE GUTIÉRREZ FAMILY
A Phoenix in Pilsen

In 1962, Emeterio and Maria Gutiérrez took over Nuevo Léon Restaurant in Chicago's Pilsen neighborhood, serving cuisine from their home in Nuevo Léon, a border state in northern Mexico. Their son Daniel started working at the restaurant in the late 1960s after serving in the U.S. Army, taking over for his father in 1986, when Emeterio passed away. When Daniel's son, Danny, entered the family business in 1989, Nuevo Léon's future seemed secure in the third generation's hands—well into the twenty-first century. But on December 2, 2015, an extra-alarm fire destroyed Nuevo Léon, leaving more than forty long-time employees without jobs and the Gutiérrez family without a business for the first time in more than fifty years. With the help of the community and the restaurant's devoted staff, the family was able to open the doors of a new restaurant, Cantón Regio, fewer than six weeks later, a testament to their resilience, their loyalty, and the Pilsen community's love for the restaurant and its northern Mexican cuisine.

On December 2, 2015, as Danny Gutiérrez was dozing off in one of the offices above Nuevo Léon Restaurant at 1515–17 West Eighteenth

43

Street, a massive fire broke out just after midnight. He woke up to a thick blanket of smoke, barely able to see through the haze. Somehow he managed to find his way down the stairs and outside, shivering in the winter air until a neighbor brought him warm clothes. "When people asked me if I was sad, or angry, or depressed, or whatever because of the fire, I said no! I was jumping up and down! Yippee! I got out alive!"

It took one hundred firefighters several hours to wrangle the flames, which destroyed the restaurant. The official report blamed the incident on faulty electrical wiring.* The fire also crept next door to Tortilleria Sabinas, a tortilla factory that has served Chicago since 1962, the same year that Danny's grandparents took over Nuevo Léon. City inspectors closed Tortilleria Sabinas the next morning, but it was deemed structurally sound later that afternoon, and corn tortillas were soon sailing down the conveyor belts, business as usual.

As the day unfolded, Danny and his father struggled to regroup. No one had been hurt, but the devastating loss registered clearly on their faces. Their immediate thoughts turned to their employees, many of whom had been working at Nuevo Léon for decades. "What am I going to do?" Danny told the *Chicago Tribune* the next morning, tears in his eyes. "I have so many people that depend on me, that depend on Nuevo Léon Restaurant."

Danny and his father immediately eyed their building across the street at 1510 West Eighteenth Street, a building that has been in the Gutiérrez family for years. Daniel operated Nayarit Nightclub there from 1986 until about 2001. The family rented the two-story space for private parties and special events after Nayarit closed, but otherwise it stood vacant, waiting for Danny to open Cantón Regio, a Mexican restaurant concept he'd been chipping away at for about ten years. Plans for Cantón Regio's opening day kept getting shoved to the back burner as Danny assumed the responsibilities of fatherhood and helping his family run Nuevo Léon, which served breakfast, lunch, and dinner, seven days a week, 365 days a year.

---

*Until 2015, Nuevo Léon operated in two buildings at 1515 and 1517 West Eighteenth Street, which were adjoined on the ground floors. Offices and apartments were on the second and third floors. The Bureau of Alcohol, Tobacco, and Firearms determined that the cause of the fire was faulty electrical wiring that ignited crawl space debris, not arson.

Above: *1515–17 West Eighteenth Street after the fire*

Left:*The rear of the building at 1515 West Eighteenth Street, where the fire started*

In the hours and days following the fire, plans to open Cantón Regio flew into action so that Danny could keep at least some of Nuevo Léon's staff on the new restaurant's payroll. Danny's other motivation was his father's happiness; Nuevo Léon had been Daniel Gutiérrez's second home for more than fifty years. "After the fire, I took one look at my father, who had lost his livelihood, and could not stand that he now had nothing to do," Danny said. "I had to get Cantón Regio up and running."

Eight in a '55 Chevy

Emeterio and Maria Gutiérrez came to Chicago in 1957 with their four sons—Tony, Matt, Daniel, and Raul—from Sabinas Hidalgo, a small town in the state of Nuevo Léon, Mexico. The family traveled with an uncle and driver, all eight packed into a 1955 Chevy. When they stopped to sleep, two would have to get out of the car to make room for the others and sleep in the grass. Construction of the interstate highway system was just getting under way, so the family took Route 66. The journey took five days.

After they arrived in Chicagoland, the Gutiérrez family lived briefly in Waukegan before moving to West Harrison Street at South Morgan, an area where many Mexican and Italian families lived until Richard J. Daley approved plans to build the UIC campus. "We lived there in a big building . . . almost all Mexican," Daniel remembered. "Sixty families lived there. Everybody that lived in that neighborhood were told they had to leave."

Restaurant ownership was never part of the plan for Emeterio, who had a job lined up at National Lead Foundry at West Forty-third and Western. He worked at the foundry during the week and Nuevo Léon on the weekends to pay for his children's education (Maria insisted that her children always attend Catholic schools). Nuevo Léon's original owner, Jose Garza, also from Nuevo Léon, grew tired of restaurant life. One day he threw in the towel and asked Emeterio if he wanted to buy the place. Emeterio and Maria Gutiérrez took over Nuevo Léon at 1515 West Eighteenth Street in March 1962 and lived on the building's second floor.

When the family arrived in Pilsen in 1962, Daniel says, the neighborhood's population was a blend of "Bohemians, Croatians, Polish, Mexican people. It was more mixed." Families were starting to move to Pilsen from Texas and Mexico—families who, like the Gutiérrezes, were drawn to the abundance of manufacturing jobs in the area. They fell in love with Maria's cooking, northern Mexican cuisine that reminded them of home.

After graduating from Cathedral High School, Daniel and two of his brothers were drafted into the U.S. Army, where Daniel served from 1966 to 1968. His eldest brother, Tony, was spared, since married men were not drafted at the time. After serving his country, Daniel was eager to get back home; he and his wife, also named Maria, were newly married and he wanted to help his parents at Nuevo Léon.

Drawing upon his uncanny ability to recall names, numbers, and dates, Daniel remembers how the Pilsen area was rife with taverns in the 1960s. "From Western to Halsted, from Eighteenth to Twenty-second, I think there were about forty-four taverns," he remembers. "They would go to 2:00 or 3:00 in the morning." In the early days, Nuevo Léon was open until 5:00 A.M. to cater to the late-night crowd. "I used to say, 'I'm waiting for the tigers to come over.' What do we get here when the people come out of the taverns at 2:00 in the morning? Rowdy. But it was good money." Over the years, the Gutiérrezes wanted to promote a family environment and started closing at 10:00 P.M. on weeknights and midnight on the weekends. Now, very few bars and even fewer taverns remain in the area.

Daniel and Maria lived in Pilsen from 1968 to 1972, before moving to Little Village to raise their family (they have four children: Letizia, Marissa, Cynthia, and Daniel Jr.). Back in the 1970s, Daniel says, people were afraid to come to Pilsen. Neighborhood kids belonged to clubs, which were synonymous with gangs. By Daniel's estimation, there were at least a dozen clubs in the Pilsen area alone. Instead of tattoos and symbols, club members wore sweaters with identifying emblems. Daniel recalls the Cullerton Boys, the Racine Boys, the Spartans. The clubs fought over history and turf. They disappeared by the 1990s and were replaced by much larger gangs such as the Latin Counts, not to be confused with the Latin Kings, originally formed in the Humboldt Park area by Puerto Ricans who came to Chicago in the 1960s (Diaz 2009).

As Nuevo Léon's business grew, the Gutiérrez family purchased the building next door at 1517 West Eighteenth Street in the 1970s and expanded with a second dining room, then expanded yet again with a third dining room in the early 1980s, for a total capacity of 180 seats. All three dining rooms were soon packed for breakfast, lunch, and dinner, seven days a week. On the weekends, a line frequently formed for breakfast, diners willingly waiting outside until a table was ready.

Throughout the restaurant's history, the menu hasn't changed much. Marcos Gonzales started coming to Nuevo Léon in 1969 and insists that the food has been consistent over the years. "The recipes don't vary," says Gonzalez, who was still bringing his family and friends to Nuevo Léon up until the days before the fire, even though he moved from the neighborhood decades before. "My parents are from the Nuevo Léon state of Mexico. What really makes the food special to me is that it's just like my mother's cooking, my grandmother's cooking."

Northern Mexican Cuisine

Northern Mexican cuisine consists primarily of meat, dairy, and products made with processed wheat instead of corn, because of its proximity to the United States. It's a diet that relies heavily on beef, with dishes like *barbacoa* (steamed beef), *caldo de res con arroz* (beef vegetable soup with rice), and *carne asada* (grilled skirt steak). There are "two ethnic groups that use *carne asada*," says Daniel, "Jewish people and Mexican people. Nobody else will touch it. It's more fatty, a fattier cut of beef."

According to Danny, "all the recipes that are on the menu are through my grandmother. Northern cuisine from Mexico." From time to time, Danny would study Nuevo Léon's long menu—about sixty items at last count—and try to weed out any dishes that didn't sell. Each time he realized the same thing: Everything sold. So everything stayed. That's why the menu has remained consistent, year after year, generation after generation.

When asked about his favorite meal from Nuevo Léon's menu, Danny was quick to respond—the *carne asada* dinner. As he checked off the

*A memorial to Emeterio Gutiérrez
at Cantón Regio*

ingredients, "skirt steak, rice, beans, some sliced avocado, some tortillas on the side . . ." he trailed off in a dreamlike state, as though just savoring his favorite meal for the first time, instead of having it within arm's reach his entire life.

Favorites on Nuevo Léon's northern Mexican menu also include *chilaquiles* and *machacado con huevo,* a breakfast dish made with flank steak that is dried, pounded, shredded by hand, and then placed in a skillet "with a little bit of oil" and scrambled with eggs. In the state of Nuevo Léon, the beef is salted and dried in the sun. On Eighteenth Street in Chicago, it's dried in-house and served with refried beans and a basket of fresh, warm tortillas. Though regulars seem to love the entire menu, if pressed, they'll name as favorites the *caldo de res con arroz*, *carne a la tampiquena* (broiled skirt steak with a cheese enchilada), *bistec a la Mexicana de lomo* (a stew of ribeye steak, tomatoes, jalapeno peppers, and onions), and *menudo* (tripe soup), a tried-and-true hangover cure.

When Danny started working at his family's restaurant in the late '80s, Nuevo Léon sourced its ingredients from the South Water Street Market at Racine and 14th Street. He remembers the old market fondly. Business owners screamed orders while merchants shouted back prices. Onions flew through the air. For a young man just entering the family business it was a heady brew of chaos and commerce. There was a deafening din from the moment the doors opened until all the food was sold, he recalls, the market emptying out until the next day's delivery before dawn.

In 2001, South Water Street Market moved to Twenty-fourth and Wolcott and was renamed the Chicago International Produce Market, a more efficient, streamlined operation offering more loading docks, online inventory, international produce, and organic foods. Nuevo Léon then started purchasing its food from both the Chicago International Produce Market and Enrique's Produce, a wholesaler on South Blue Island.

Other than corn tortillas, which are sourced from the local tortillerias Sabinas and El Milagro, Nuevo Léon's food has always been made in-house from scratch, from the chorizo to the *machacado* to their signature mole sauce, a Mexican tradition that originated in the Mexican state of Puebla.

Mole Poblano

Mole is a labor-intensive sauce made with varied combinations of dried chilis, spices, seeds, nuts, chocolate, fruit, chicken broth, and thickeners such as pieces of torn bread or tortilla strips. No matter which other ingredients are used, it's the chocolate that gives mole its rich, velvety character. Different regions of Mexico produce different types of mole, including red, green, and black, even white. But Nuevo Léon has only focused on one: poblano.

"Mole is underappreciated," Danny says. "Most people do not know how much hard work goes into it." Nuevo Léon's version, which contains about twenty-four ingredients, won the People's Choice Award at the 2015 Mole de Mayo, an annual mole contest held in Pilsen with "arts, music, and mucho mole." With the help of staff and family members, Danny served about 200 pounds of his grandmother's recipe during the two-day fest. The sauce takes about eight hours to make, with father and son presiding over it, coaxing each batch until perfect. One bite into Nuevo Léon's *pollo en mole*, an entree of steamed chicken, beans, rice, and mole poblano, reveals the sauce's complexity, an earthy mixture at once smoky, sweet, and intense, with just a hint of heat. There's really nothing else like it anywhere.

One day Daniel Sr. mused, "Does Rick Bayless make mole?"

Daniel Jr.: "He probably makes mango mole."

No Coolers or Hard Liquor

I first crossed paths with the Gutiérrez family while writing *BYOB Chicago*, a guide to the bring-your-own-bottle dining scene in Chicagoland. Nuevo Léon has been a mainstay on Chicago's BYOB map ever since the practice of bringing your own alcohol to a restaurant became popular.

It is challenging for a restaurant to stay in business without alcohol sales. Despite this opportunity for increased profits, Nuevo Léon has never held a liquor license. It was Emeterio who established this policy, firmly stating that *his* restaurant would never serve liquor—period. To him, alcohol meant problematic behavior, and he never wanted his staff to endure drunk, rude customers. Many BYOB restaurateurs also fear that staff will overindulge if they stock alcohol, preferring to focus on the food and let customers choose their own wine or beer. Although they're aware of the revenue potential, Daniel and Danny have honored Emeterio's wishes—at both Nuevo Léon and Cantón Regio. For them, tradition trumps profit when it comes to the family business. It also means higher turnover. "If I have liquor, I have a table there," said Daniel, gesturing to a table nearby, "they're going to be there for two hours. If they just come to eat, they'll be here forty-five minutes. In and out. In and out."

Customers have never complained about Nuevo Léon's BYOB policy. In fact, it was commonplace to see customers coming in with a six-pack swinging from their hands or a bottle of wine in tow. People used to bring in hard liquor, doing shots of tequila with abandon. I remember coming in one day and seeing a blender at a table, a customer whipping up margaritas for a large party. Some even wheeled in coolers of beer. Nuevo Léon responded to the debauchery by posting a policy: No hard liquor. No coolers. Limit three beers per person. Several BYOBs have instituted similar limits when customers abuse their BYOB policies. It was a move the Gutiérrezes were reluctant to make, though it was necessary to preserve the stable environment that Emeterio envisioned for his business.

The History of "Little Pilsen"

Some of the Gutiérrez family still live in Pilsen, which is about two and a half miles southwest of the Loop. It was originally named "Little Plzeň" in 1870 after one of the largest cities in Bohemia, now the Czech Republic.

Pilsen is bordered on the south by the Chicago River; the north by a series of railroad yards and viaducts referred to by locals as "The Wall"; the west by somewhere between Ashland and Western avenues, depending on the source; and the east by Canal Street. Within Pilsen are Gads Hill, Heart of Chicago, and Heart of Italy. The central nerve is the intersection of Eighteenth Street, Blue Island, and Loomis Street, where a plaza hosts a constant hive of activity.

Bohemians came to Chicago in the middle of the nineteenth century, settling in Pilsen after Chicago Mayor Wentworth used the force of the Chicago police to purge them from the North Side. Known as the Battle of the Sands, this ugly spot on Chicago's history proved fortuitous for the Bohemians, as Pilsen dodged the Great Chicago Fire of 1871. In need of new facilities after the fire, many large industries moved to Pilsen, which became a thriving manufacturing and transportation hub for lumber, coal, farm equipment, and beer. By 1875 thousands of Bohemians lived in Pilsen. St. Procopius Church at 1651 South Allport was originally established in 1875 as a Bohemian parish (Saclarides 2009).

The Bohemian city of Plzeň is famous for pilsner, a style of pale lager beer now well-known throughout the world. Several large breweries were established in Chicago's Pilsen in the nineteenth and early twentieth centuries, including Bohemian Brewing Co., which morphed into Atlas Brewing; Pilsen Brewing; and Peter Schoenhofen Brew Company. Judge and Dolph Company, a rum, whisky, and gin distributor purchased by Wirtz Beverage Illinois (now Breakthru Beverage Group), was based in Pilsen on Cermak Road in the early 1900s (Pero 2011, 13–24).

Pilsen's history of promoting community activism and social justice began with its Bohemian residents. In 1877, the neighborhood was at the epicenter of a national railroad strike, with workers fighting for better pay and working conditions. The U.S. Army marched into Pilsen to fight Bohemian, Irish, and Polish workers in the Battle of the Viaduct at Halsted and Sixteenth streets, killing thirty and wounding one hundred. Although no marker commemorates the site, it's known as the bloodiest street battle in U.S. labor history (Pero 2011, 18–19; WTTW 2013).

As successive waves of immigrants moved to Pilsen at the turn of the twentieth century in search of lower-cost housing and better business opportunities, settlement houses and missions were established to deal with the social problems of overcrowding. Pilsen's Howell House, originally formed in 1909 by the Presbyterian Church as a community outreach center, was modeled after Chicago's Hull House (Pero 2011, 103). By the 1920s, Pilsen's population, then a mix of Czechs, Irish, Germans, Poles, Slovaks, Lithuanians, Italians, and Croatians, swelled to 85,000 (Pero, 25).

During the middle of the twentieth century, Pilsen became a port of entry for Mexican immigrants, who also sought better economic conditions and improved job opportunities. The nearby South Lawndale area, or Little Village, was also a magnet for Mexican immigrants. The Mexican population in Little Village–Pilsen catapulted from 6,972 in 1960 to 83,385 in 1980 and to about 109,000 in 1990 (Casuso and Camacho 1995, 358).

Chicago, of course, has since become famous for having one of the largest Mexican populations in the country. Of all U.S. metropolitan areas, Chicagoland has the fourth largest Mexican population, behind Los Angeles; Riverside, California; and Houston (Pew Research Center 2016). There are approximately two million Hispanics in Chicago's metropolitan region; more than 1.5 million are Mexican, representing over 16 percent of Chicagoland's entire population (U.S. Census Bureau 2010).

Pilsen's Combined Heritage

The sights, sounds, flavors, and architecture of Pilsen are a blend of its European origins and more recent Hispanic influences. The welcome sign at Thalia Hall, an arts center built by John Dusek in 1892, is in three languages: Bohemian, Spanish, and Italian. Saint Procopius conducts Sunday Mass in English, Croatian, and Spanish. And in 1965, Howell House passed on its buildings at 1831 South Racine to Casa Aztlán, an organization designed to assist the Mexican community (Pero 2011, 108). Casa Aztlan lost this property in 2013 to a real estate developer, who painted over the iconic murals by artist Ray Patlan. This provoked an outcry from the Pilsen community, which prizes its storied murals, some of which are decades old. (The developer has since vowed to bring Patlan back to create a new mural on the building.)

Pilsen's multitude of murals is perhaps its strongest calling card, making it a destination for many who are drawn to this Mexican art form. Murals proliferate Pilsen's landscape, from the sides of buildings to CTA stations to schools, bathing the area with warm, vibrant colors and narratives steeped in history and politics. Pilsen's schools carry on this tradition through art apprenticeships that teach students how to create murals.

The Mexican mural movement came to Pilsen in the 1970s with such artists as Francisco Mendoza and Jose Gonzalez, who brought the art form to Chicago after Gonzalez's teacher at Notre Dame refused to take Mexican art seriously. Gonzalez also introduced Chicagoans to Mexico's traditional *Dia de los muertos* (Day of the dead) at a River North gallery in 1983 (Pridmore 1991). This has become an annual tradition in which residents set out favorite liquors and foods to prepare for a visit from their dearly departed. Pilsen is also known for its annual reenactment of the Crucifixion every Holy Friday, *El dia de los niños*, or Children's Day, every April, and the wildly popular street festival *Fiesta del sol* every August.

"It's a better community than it was in the '70s," Daniel said in 2017. "People are not afraid to walk the streets. This is a neighborhood where you want to come and live *right now*," he said emphatically. "Right now, at the present."

Eighteenth Street now teems with a constant flow of pedestrian and street traffic. Push-cart vendors peddle *paletas,* Mexican ice pops, in a variety of flavors. Sellers hawk Mexican trinkets on the sidewalk in front of high-traffic taquerias. Traditional Mexican bakeries like La Baguette mingle with bars adorned with neon craft-brewery signs. The air is thick with native Spanish, steam rising from taco carts, music blaring from open-air bars. English-speaking newcomers stroll with babies and dogs, enjoying the relative calm that now envelops the neighborhood. Residents enjoy food truck fests, block parties, a game of hoops. Children benefit from after-school programs offered at Rudy Lozano Chicago Public Library, which houses one of the largest collections of Spanish-language books in the Midwest.

While the media has reported local distaste for gentrification and its threat to Pilsen's ethnic heritage and affordable housing options, many embrace the change and investments coming into the area. The neighborhood, Daniel attests, has changed a lot, but the changes are good. Business in Pilsen is great, he says—for him and for others. He spots groups of school children regularly visiting Pilsen to admire the murals and to soak in the neighborhood's rich history.

Daniel Sr., the Mayor of Pilsen

A couple of days after the fire in 2015, Nuevo Léon's employees gathered on Eighteenth Street to survey the wreckage, comfort each other, and provide solace to Daniel, the restaurant's second-generation owner and modern-day patriarch. On a cold, sunny winter day, the group huddled together, chanting expressions of family, love, and devotion to their long-time employer, though many would bristle at that term. The Gutiérrez family, their employees, and even their customers have always acted like a tight-knit, devoted family, a rarity in the restaurant business, an industry vulnerable to high turnover and snarky Yelp reviews.

Before Nuevo Léon burned down I was able to speak with some of the employees who had worked there for decades, employees who have since found jobs elsewhere. They were eager to shower the Gutiérrezes with praise.

Gloria Flores, a petite, slightly reserved woman originally from Mexico City, worked for the Gutiérrez family from 1972 until 2015. Even after working an eight-hour shift, she was happy to sit down with me and share what working at Nuevo Léon meant to her. "Daniel Sr. told us, 'As long as you act like a professional, you will always have me behind you for support. I'd prefer to lose a bad customer than a good employee,'" she offered. "He requires a lot of discipline and professionalism from us. But he will always back us up if there's ever any conflict between a customer and an employee. He cares for us, and that's one of the biggest reasons why I stay here so long."

Margarita Hernandez, who was a server from 1989 to 2015, joined Flores as we spoke, nodding enthusiastically in agreement with her long-time colleague. Originally from Pachuca, Hidalgo, Hernandez told me how Daniel "treats us like his own family, but he demands respect, professionalism, and discipline. Those two things never get confused," she said in a rapid stream of Spanish, the primary language spoken at both Nuevo Léon and Cantón Regio.

Throughout the years, Nuevo Léon's staff commonly celebrated ten, twenty, even thirty years of employment. One server, Esperanza, retired after forty-five years of service. "I hired her after I got out of the Army," said Daniel. "She was here before Daniel Jr. was born." Long-time customers asked for their favorite servers by name—even waiting for a table if their section was full.

As employers and employees collected on the sidewalk, hugging and crying two days after the fire, it was hard to tell who was comforting whom.

Post-Fire: The Community Rallies

News of the fire spread throughout the community within minutes. Community activist Jorge Valdivia once worked in Pilsen and was a long-time, devoted Nuevo Léon patron. Valdivia learned of the fire on social media and immediately saw the need for help. "I was watching a lot of the comments posted on Facebook, and there was a moment when I realized that people wanted to do something, and they wanted to channel their grief." Valdivia reached out to the Gutiérrez family and offered to help organize a Christmas party for the employees on December 22. "They loved the idea. I think it was organized within a matter of two-and-a-half to three weeks. Relatively quickly. That's the power of a community coming together and being there for one another."

Valdivia secured event space from his former employer, the National Museum of Mexican Art, and then created a Facebook page to centralize efforts for the event. Local businesses such as Dusek's and El Milagro offered to help with donations of food, toys, or anything else that was needed. A wholesaler donated meat—enough to feed the entire staff and their families. Nuevo Léon on Twenty-sixth Street, owned by Daniel's brother Matt Gutiérrez, offered to cook it. Offers of employment came pouring in from local businesses. Freddie's in Bridgeport, Los Delfines seafood restaurant, and Tomate Fresh Kitchen all offered holiday or permanent employment to staff members who found themselves out of work—an especially tough predicament so close to the holidays. "It was just incredible," said Valdivia, who was overwhelmed by the outpouring of donations from small local businesses. Univision reported the event, as did Fox News and WGN Radio. The Eighteenth Street Development Corporation raised thousands of dollars with a GoFundMe campaign, which was distributed to employees.

"Nuevo Léon is about more than the food," said Valdivia. "It's about the history of a community. It's where different generations of different families came together and shared meals, whether after Mass or in the middle of the week. It's where friendships thrived, where colleagues met for lunch. It was a ritual for some people. There are many stories out there about how families came together and shared meals and how that should be something that we should celebrate more. I think that Nuevo Léon is where the community came together."

At the employee party, Daniel worked the room, like he has for so many years at Nuevo Léon, decked out in a red sweatshirt covered in handwritten messages—a gift from his staff. "He was so happy to be there. It was emotional for him," said Valdivia. "I think he was at peace, being able to see his employees and their families celebrate Christmas." Employees are like family, Daniel says over and over, a mantra his father taught him.

Meanwhile, hundreds of loyal customers flocked to Nuevo Léon's Facebook page, offering their condolences and sharing memories. Memories of birthdays, baptisms, first dates at Nuevo Léon. Loving memories of Nuevo Léon's cofounder, Maria *Abuelita* Gutiérrez, who was stationed at the restaurant until she passed away in 2009. Comments poured in from people, many desperate to know when their beloved restaurant was reopening. The family reassured everyone that Nuevo Léon would reopen in "the next year or so" but to check out their new place, Cantón Regio, which translates to "northern home."

Cantón Regio: Third Generation on Eighteenth Street

On January 8, 2016, with the smell of smoke still lingering in the air, Danny was able to open Cantón Regio, his father working right alongside him, just like Daniel Sr. and Daniel Jr. have done for so many years. Online chatter suggested that Cantón Regio would be "Nuevo Léon II" or "Nuevo Latino." Cantón Regio is neither. The food is 100 percent authentic northern Mexican cuisine, but Cantón Regio was borne out of a concept quite different from Nuevo Léon's. Instead of tacos, tostadas, and fajitas, Cantón Regio's pared-down menu focuses on mesquite-smoked chicken, grilled steak "by the kilo," and skewers of shrimp, chicken, steak, and veggies.

Danny gave me a tour of his new restaurant's space shortly after opening day, pointing to antiques and artifacts he had collected over the years. "These were all in boxes," he said, pointing to his grandfather's horse saddle, which hangs above the stairwell leading to the lofted dining area, as well as four actual street signs from Nuevo Léon, Mexico, which he traded with local officials for a bottle of Don Julio tequila. Furniture, wrought-iron chandeliers, antique poster art, and horseshoes, repurposed into coat hooks, were all brought out of storage immediately to prepare for what might be one of the fastest restaurant openings in Chicago.

Danny hired about twenty people to staff Cantón Regio—cooks and servers who all worked together at Nuevo Léon for "years." A former Nuevo Léon cook, who had moved on to Uncle Julio's on North Avenue, came back to help out for the opening. "A customer came in and asked me, 'How long have you been open?'" Danny said. "I said, 'We just opened yesterday.' He said, 'Really? Your staff runs like a well-oiled machine!' He couldn't believe how well everything ran. That's because all of these people worked together for many years across the street."

I have sat back and witnessed Cantón Regio's staff many times, marveling at how incredibly hard they all work. So many people have asked me, "Why has the Gutiérrez family been in business on Eighteenth Street for so many decades?" One of the reasons is their staff. I simply find them some of the hardest working and most gracious people I have ever met. When I think about their work ethic and loyalty, however, it is with a touch of bittersweet. Because I know, deep in my heart, that this level of professionalism and dedication is a rare and endangered species in the hospitality industry.

Cantón Regio is not without its drawbacks. Danny misses being more hands-on with the food in Nuevo Léon's larger kitchen. Cantón Regio's small, open kitchen is limited. In fact, it's amazing that they produce as much food as they do, using every square inch of space to crank out breakfast, lunch, and dinner service. Staff do all the prep work in the basement, hoisting trays of food up and down the narrow stairs throughout their shifts.

And locals miss Nuevo Léon's menu. A few months after opening, Cantón Regio started serving breakfast at Daniel's behest, bringing back *machacado con huevo*, *huevo rancheros*, and *chilaquiles*, to the delight of Nuevo Léon's long-time regulars. Some of them had been coming to Nuevo Léon for three generations, according to Daniel, who greets everyone at the door and roams the floor, table-hopping and chatting with his constituency. "They're third-generation customers. I love to see that. And I know a lot of people by name."

"My father is very good at remembering names," Danny chimed in. "First *and* last names."

Former Nuevo Léon customers account for about half of Cantón Regio's business during the day and a little less at night, says Danny, the rest coming in from all over Chicagoland, particularly drawn to the now-legendary grilled steak. An all-male staff buzz around Cantón Regio's 115-seat space in sharp, all-black uniforms, their T-shirts emblazoned with descriptions of the new restaurant's brand: *autentico*, *tradicional*, *sabroso*, and *norteño* (authentic, traditional, delicious, and northern).

A year after opening day, Danny was still fielding calls from people, asking if this new restaurant was "just like Nuevo Léon." He patiently described the new menu, pointing out its similarities and differences. They also wanted to know, "When is Nuevo Léon reopening?"

If the family decides to reopen Nuevo Léon, it most likely would be on the first and second floors of a new building at 1515 West Eighteenth Street. The 1517 West Eighteenth Street building, which Emeterio and Maria purchased in the 1970s to expand with a second dining room, was handed down to their son Raul, who passed away two months after the fire. Raul's eight children have inherited the property from his estate and will determine its future.

Daniel has been encouraged to reopen Nuevo Léon on the South Side or other areas in Chicago. But he has no desire to run a family business anywhere but Eighteenth Street. Even though he and his wife have lived in North Riverside for decades, Daniel refers to Eighteenth Street and Pilsen as "his neighborhood." It is the place that has nurtured and sustained his family for so long. It is his home.

The Future

Each time I visited the original Nuevo Léon, I always looked up at the portrait of Maria Gutiérrez, which hung over the cash register. It was painted for the Gutiérrez family by long-time customer Carlos Medina and was destroyed in the fire, along with photos, team trophies, and mementos that can never be replaced.

When Nuevo Léon's building was destroyed, Danny was kicked out of the proverbial nest and given the opportunity to pursue his own dream, his own business. The décor, the uniforms, the menu, the plating at Cantón Regio—these details may have been greatly inspired by his ancestors, but they are of his execution. Danny's son, also named Daniel, the fourth generation in the Chicago Gutiérrez family, runs around his father's restaurant on his days off from school. "I'm starting him out young," Danny jokes.

It's not always easy, carrying on the legacy of a family restaurant. Restaurant ownership is fraught with both risk and reward. Danny and his father know this firsthand, citing the long hours and personal demands required to keep the family business going. Yet they also appreciate the benefits. According to Danny, "Seeing other families celebrate birthdays, graduations, communions, and baptisms, and being able to share that with them, throughout many years and many generations . . . It's rewarding for both of us, seeing families grow up here."

The Gutiérrez family takes care of each other; that is without question. Economics, identity, and new generations will continue to drive the unfolding of this family's future on Eighteenth Street. It is a future that is as uncertain as it is certain.

Chicago: The Tortilla Factory Capital

The next time you see tortillas at the local grocery, take a look at the back of the package. Chances are they were made in Chicago. Chicago boasts a surprising number of tortilla factories—the most artisanal corn tortilla factories in the world, according to some. Although the Gutiérrez family makes their own flour tortillas, they purchase corn tortillas from two producers in Chicago's Pilsen/Little Village area: Sabinas and El Milagro.

Sabinas Food Products, Inc., is across the street from Cantón Regio at 1509 West Eighteenth Street. Open since 1962, the same year the Gutiérrez family took over Nuevo Léon, this tortilla factory is named after the Gutiérrez family's home town in Nuevo Léon, Mexico. It produces varieties of tortilla products and distributes them to restaurants, retailers, and wholesalers, making all of their products from 100 percent stone-ground corn.

Sabinas does not offer public tours, but they do sell products to the public near the entrance of the factory. Walk-ins can purchase three different styles of kettle-cooked tortilla chips (salted restaurant-style, unsalted homestyle, and spicy homestyle), all of which are made with yellow corn, corn oil, salt, and a trace of lime. Also available are fresh tortillas—so fresh they steam up the bag—and *masa*, a corn dough folks use to press their own tortillas at home.

El Milagro, which has multiple locations in Chicagoland, Atlanta, and Texas, was established in Chicago in the 1950s and manufactures a wide array of tortilla products, including chips, tostada shells, burrito wraps, fajita wraps, and taco shells. All are made with either yellow corn, white corn, white flour, or wheat flour. El Milagro is well-known for its traditional six-inch corn tortillas, which sell by the dozen at most retailers for under a dollar.

Besides Sabinas and El Milagro, there is also El Popocatepetl, a tortilla factory with locations in Pilsen and Archer Heights. Established in 1964 by Jose Avina, El Popocatepetl, or "El Popo," was named after an active volcano in central Mexico. Avina passed the business on to his nephews Ernesto and Jose Avina, brothers who split sometime during the 1970s, with Ernesto retaining El Popo and Jose moving on to Sabinas. Ernesto's daughters Yvonne and Elizabeth Avina have since taken over the factory, which distributes tortillas to local restaurants such as Big Star, Frontera Grill, and Hub 51. Locals flock to El Popo's *tortillerias* during Christmas and New Year's, when masa is traditionally used for homemade tortillas and tamales.

Three Facts about Corn Tortillas Made in Chicago

What exactly is "stone-ground corn"?

If it says "stone-ground corn" on the label, it means the company uses real, whole corn in the cooking process. According to Yvonne Avina, co-owner of El Popocatepetl Tortillas, many tortilla factories in Chicago cook their corn like El Popo, with stone-ground corn. In other areas around the country, manufacturers just open up a bag of corn flour, mix it with water, and make tortillas. El Popo cooks the corn and grinds it into masa at the factory. They use stones with various cuts to achieve a more finely ground corn. Stone-ground corn affects the texture of the tortilla.

What is masa?

Masa is a corn dough. It is used to make tortillas.

Authentic corn tortillas are made with only three ingredients: corn, water, and trace of lime. What is the lime used for?

According to Avina, the lime is used as a preservative. It is actually limestone, not lime fruit. A food grade lime, it is also used in the cooking process to soften the hardest part of the corn and break up the corn's pH content. Lime also brings out the *amarilla*, or yellow color of the corn.

Caldo de res (Beef vegetable soup)

Many of Nuevo Léon and Cantón Regio's customers order this hearty, subtly seasoned soup for breakfast, though it is served all day. This northern Mexican recipe was handed down from Maria Gutiérrez, who took over Nuevo Léon with her husband, Emeterio, in 1962. The Gutiérrez family serves caldo de res with a side of rice and lime wedges. It calls for a large portion of bone-in cuts of meat. To modify, reduce the portions of meat or purchase boneless cuts. Trust the steps involved; this recipe has worked for decades.

Serves 8–12

Ingredients

6 lbs. beef shank meat
2 lbs. choice beef short rib
4 lbs. beef hind shank, bone in

Nuevo Léon seasoning:
  ½ tsp. powdered garlic
  ½ tsp. black pepper
  ¼ tsp. cumin
  Salt to taste

4 carrots, sliced
4 cobs of corn, cut into thirds

2 stalks celery, sliced
4 medium-sized potatoes, cubed
3 zucchini, sliced
2 bell peppers, diced
½ white onion, sliced
1 small can (14.5–15 oz.) tomato sauce
2 fresh tomatoes, diced
½ head of cabbage, cut into pieces
½ bunch cilantro, chopped
Long-grain rice (*optional*)

Directions

1. Rinse all meat of blood, etc. Place all meat in large stock pot, add water until meat is covered. Bring to boil for 15 minutes. Add Nuevo Léon seasoning mix.

2. Cook for an additional 45 minutes, keeping at a boil.

3. Add carrots, corn, celery to pot. Cook for about 30 minutes or until tender.

4. Add potatoes, zucchini, peppers, onion, tomato sauce, fresh tomatoes, cabbage, and cilantro. Cook for an additional 15 minutes.

5. Salt to taste throughout cooking.

6. Serve immediately with rice.

Four

THE PARTHENON
An Anchor in Greektown

Filoxenia is a Greek term for the ancient tradition of hospitality. Literally meaning "love of strangers," filoxenia is a generosity of spirit, an expression of the-best-of-what's-mine-is-yours attitude in which Greeks take great pride. At the Parthenon, the Liakouras family embodied the essence of filoxenia for forty-eight years. Owner Chris Liakouras was a constant thread throughout the restaurant's history, greeting customers at the entrance from the day it opened on July 5, 1968, until it closed unexpectedly in September 2016. The restaurant's enormous contributions to Chicago and Greektown certainly warrant a place in culinary history. The interviews for this chapter were conducted before The Parthenon lit its last plate of saganaki and cried its final burst of "Opaa!"

Like many dyed-in-the-wool Chicagoans, I will admit that I have grown wary of places that boast the distinction of being the tallest, oldest, or first of anything. The Parthenon Restaurant, at 314 South Halsted Street in Chicago's Greektown, claimed to be the birthplace of flaming *saganaki*, the famous cheese dish now known throughout the world. Until they closed in 2016, they also claimed to be the oldest restaurant in Chicago's Greektown. You may have also heard that the Parthenon was instrumental in the widespread popularity across America of gyros.* Big-city blustering, we Chicagoans might think. But it didn't take more than one or two visits to this Greektown institution to realize two things about the Parthenon: (1) people simply came here for the food, not any marketing gimmicks; and (2) all of these claims appear to be true.

Brothers Chris and Bill Liakouras opened The Parthenon in 1968, giving it the distinction of being the oldest restaurant in Greektown throughout its forty-eight-year run. (The second oldest is Greek Islands, which opened in 1971.) Though Bill returned to Greece in 1976, Chris worked at front of house for the nearly fifty years the restaurant was open. With his towering frame, warm smile, and gracious manner, he was a familiar face to many. Even in the restaurant's final days, Chris, by then in his eighties, was at the entrance, answering the phone, dealing with vendors, and greeting customers—usually by name.

During its tenure, the Parthenon weathered the dramatic economic and demographic changes in Greektown, a neighborhood centered on a strip of Halsted between Monroe and Van Buren. Chicago's original Greektown, referred to as the Delta, was bounded by Harrison, Polk, Halsted, and Blue Island. The Delta was razed in the 1960s to make way for the expressways and the UIC campus.

Chris didn't think he held any special secrets for staying in business for so long. He was adamant, however, about one thing: the quality of his food had top priority. "The customers have to like the food, number one, because they come out to eat, you understand?" he said in his still-thick Greek accent, sipping on his ever-present glass of chamomile tea. "Hugging and kissing, that's fine, but the food has to be good. No other place in the world has the gyros that we make," he said matter-of-factly. At that claim, your inner skeptic might rear its head again—unless you've tried the Parthenon's gyros.

The Parthenon Perfects Gyros

Gyros originated in Greece, where they were made with meat scraps and fillers. They were first introduced in America by Greek restaurants

---

*The correct way to pronounce *gyros*: 'yē-ˌrōs.

68

in Chicago—places like Gyros, the Parthenon's original name before Chris and Bill purchased it. The previous owner's namesake dish was too salty, and it didn't sell very well, Chris said. But the Liakouras brothers kept Gyros's chef, Angelo Gailas, recognizing talent in the Athens native. Chris worked with Gailas to perfect what became one of the Parthenon's trademark dishes—freshly made gyros, a healthier, tastier alternative to the rotating cones of mystery meat peddled at most fast food joints.

The Parthenon's gyros were made with a combination of 85 percent pure beef and 15 percent pure lamb. "We get our lamb from Colorado," said Chris. "It is more expensive than other sources, but it is fresh and it is the best." The meat was ground, seasoned, and then refrigerated for a few hours to set. "Cooks better this way," Chris insisted. No marinade used, just freshly ground meat, salt, pepper, and herbs. Every morning, the kitchen created fresh batches of gyros, then pressed seventy pounds of the mixture onto each of the gyros machines in an inverted cone shape. Why this shape? I asked Chris one day, expecting to hear a long-kept secret about a gadget I'd seen my entire life but never knew much about. Chris just shrugged, offering that "it simply looks better" in his typically unpretentious, affable manner.

Even people who worked in other Greektown restaurants came to the Parthenon for the made-to-order gyros, which were never made with frozen meat. They were succulent, juicy, and perfectly seasoned. Only a handful of places in Chicago make fresh gyros in-house. It's a costlier, more time-consuming method, said Dino Sakkas, whose father, George Sakkas, ran Gyros on a Spit in Lakeview for twenty-seven years. Dino revitalized his father's recipes for fresh gyros at a second Gyros on a Spit in Lincoln Park, which had a three-year run until it closed in early 2017. His customers would go to the Parthenon when Gyros on a Spit was closed, said Dino. The younger Sakkas sees a growing demand for unprocessed food and natural ingredients, and he's still hoping that demand for freshly made gyros will grow.

When the Parthenon first opened, Chris and Bill sourced their gyros machines from Greece. These ran on electricity and constantly shorted out. After spending yet another day fiddling with a broken machine, he and Bill conspired with a metalworker and the gas company to figure out how to build a better gyros machine. The result? A larger, more reliable device that used gas burners. Visible from the restaurant's front windows, these workhorses cooked millions of pounds of gyros, one sizzling and crackling cone at a time, up until the Parthenon's very last day in business.

The Parthenon's unique gyro machines

The Parthenon's gyros machines did not automatically rotate like others, which cook the meat unevenly, said Chris. Instead, the Parthenon's gyros machines cooked the meat facing the burners, which took about five to ten minutes. A trained chef then manually rotated the cone and sliced the cooked meat down. Each side was cooked and sliced, cooked and sliced, until there was nothing left on the cone. The Parthenon eschewed electric knives and cut the gyros slices manually. This gave it a more homemade look, said Chris.

Chris and Bill were awarded a patent on their innovation in 1968. It expired in 1973, the five-year maximum due to what Chris understood as the patent's "usefulness to consumers." Companies like Central Gyros Wholesale, Grecian Delight, and Kronos Foods Inc., all of which were founded in Chicago in the 1970s, jumped in to mass-produce gyros machines and cones, making Chicago the largest gyros manufacturing area. With little in common with the Parthenon's version but the name, factory-produced gyros are made with ground beef and lamb trimmings, fillers, and other preservatives, shaped into bandage-colored tubes on assembly lines, then frozen and shipped around the country (Segal 2009).

When he opened the Parthenon, Chris was so eager to share his new version of gyros that he handed out free samples to all his customers, along with complimentary bites of one of his other innovations: flaming saganaki.

The Saganaki Story

When I was growing up in the northwest suburbs of Chicago, we would go out to eat at one of the many Greek-owned restaurants in the area. Ordering flaming saganaki and watching the flames shoot toward the ceiling transformed a regular meal into a celebratory evening out. It dictated which outfit I wore. Little did I know as a kid that the birthplace of this festive dish was mere miles away at Halsted and Jackson.

Flaming saganaki is fried cheese doused with a splash of brandy and ignited with a cigarette lighter and a quick flick of the wrist. A night at the Parthenon was not complete without at least one order, always accompanied by an exclamation of "Opaa!"* Chris was happy to share the well-worn but charming story of how he created his version of saganaki, which is now served throughout the United States and other parts of the world.

Like gyros, saganaki originated in Greece. There restaurants take a piece of kasseri, a salty cheese, fry it in a pan, and serve it on a regular, cold plate. It is served as an appetizer, a common part of any Greek meal. During one of their morning sessions developing the menu, Chris and his head chef, Gailas, took kasseri, which melts slowly and is commonly compared to provolone, dipped it in a batter of milk and egg, coated it in flour, then fried it in olive oil. They served it in the sizzling pan in which it was fried, squeezing lemon on the smoking cheese to cool it down as it arrived at the customer's

---

*Chris Liakouras defines *opaa!* as "an expression, like when you are dancing, having fun."

table. This preparation and presentation is completely different from the original version in Greece, Chris explained.

A few days after the Parthenon opened, a group of women came in to see Chris, who waited on them when he and Bill worked at Diana's Grocery and Restaurant at 310 South Halsted. Chris brought over sample plates of gyros and saganaki to his table of regulars, eager for their reaction. When he put the smoking plate of cheese on the table, one of the women said, "Why don't you put a little brandy on it and light it up? Make a little show of it?" Ever the gracious host, Chris obliged, grabbing a bottle of Metaxa (Greek brandy) and setting off the first plume of flaming saganaki, much to the women's delight.

Chris immediately changed the menu item from "saganaki" to "flaming saganaki," instructing his only waiter at the time, George, to carefully practice igniting the hot plate of cheese, warning him to not set his hair on fire. George started using Cognac, as Metaxa can be quite expensive, got a lighter out of his pocket, and cried "Opaa!" "We didn't invent the word 'saganaki,'" reminded Chris. "We just invented the way to make it different." I asked Chris whether anyone has ever set anything on fire while preparing flaming saganaki at the Parthenon, aside from the time in the '60s he set his own hair aflame (the moment is captured in a photo that hung near the restaurant's entrance). Just once in almost fifty years, he said. It happened with the only female server ever hired at the Parthenon; her hair, too, caught on fire. Considering the size of the flame and volume of flaming saganaki served over forty-eight years, I consider this an amazing accomplishment in itself.

The birthplace of flaming saganaki is not without controversy. Some sources say that Petros Kogeones, who owned Diana's, Dianna's Opaa, and Petros Dianna's—all located on Halsted—was the first person to flame kasseri cheese with Greek brandy (Ganakos 2005), or that Diana's was the first restaurant to serve it, maybe even by Chris, who used to wait tables there.

After hearing that Petros Kogeones was alive and well and still living in Chicago, I gave him a call. I had heard quite a bit about Petros and his brother Peter, after whom an honorary stretch of South Halsted is named. Norbert Blei wrote about Petros in *Chi Town*, describing him as "a modern Greek myth of his own making" who was famous for

Chris Liakouras with flaming saganaki (and hair)

dancing while balancing a glass of wine on his head and always being surrounded by a lot of women (Blei 2003).

Kogeones declined to say anything specific when I asked him about the origins of flaming saganaki. He simply stated that he addressed the controversy years ago and that it no longer mattered, as he was no longer in the business. Before hanging up, he parted with a genteel "All right, my love. Thank you."

George J. Gekas, who published cookbooks containing recipes from traditional Greek restaurants in Chicago, New York, and Detroit, included the Parthenon's recipe for flaming saganaki in his 1991 cookbook *Opaa! Greek Cooking Chicago Style*. Though Gekas did add that the Parthenon "claims" creation of the dish, its inclusion is a nod to the Parthenon's legacy. Long-time Greektown restaurateurs and staff at the National Hellenic Museum on Halsted maintain that they did not see flaming saganaki anywhere before the Parthenon, and that the Parthenon's reputation as the birthplace of flaming saganaki is cemented far outside of Chicago (Johnson 2014).

The Parthenon's Recipes—A Legacy

In the Parthenon's nearly fifty-year history, only two head chefs manned its kitchen—Angelo Gailas and Sotirios Stasinos. Gailas opened the Parthenon with the Liakouras brothers on July 5, 1968, and worked with Chris to fine-tune the recipes that dominated the menu throughout its history. Gailas started training Stasinos in 1976, when the seventeen-year-old wandered into the restaurant looking for work. Gailas was tough on his charge, knowing that he wasn't just teaching him how to cook—he was handing down a legacy. It took several years, Chris said, for Gailas to train Stasinos, who took over the kitchen in the early 1980s.* This level of devotion ensured that the Parthenon's time-honored recipes were passed down from generation to generation. (Several of these recipes have also been preserved in *The Parthenon Cookbook*, by Camille Stagg).

The dish I will miss the most at the Parthenon is spanakopita, or spinach pie. I've conducted extensive empirical research on this dish.

---

*After The Parthenon closed, Stasinos filed a complaint in December 2016 accusing the Liakourases of breach of fiduciary duty.

Since I was a kid, I have ordered spinach pie wherever and whenever I can, addicted to the flaky phyllo dough and tangy feta cheese. The Parthenon's entrée version, like the rest of the menu, easily stretched to at least two meals. The delicate phyllo was perfectly browned and crisped, and the fresh herbs brightened the spinach and feta filling. This singular dish, in my mind, embodied the Parthenon. It not only demonstrated the great care with which their ingredients were sourced and selected but also reflected how the traditional Greek recipes were carefully handed down from one generation to the next.

Besides gyros, saganaki, and spanakopita, Gailas and Chris also developed recipes for lemon artichokes, all of the Parthenon's lamb dishes, moussaka, pastitsio, and dolmas. Stasinos added some of his own recipes during his tenure, including the chicken *spanaki*, or chicken stuffed with spinach and feta. Regulars came on Wednesdays for the restaurant's famous navy bean soup, among them Billy Goat Tavern's owner Sam Sianis (son of founder "Billy Goat" Sianis). He came to the Parthenon every Wednesday and ate two bowls of soup, said Chris, who was an old friend. "He was the best man at my wedding with Lorraine," said Chris. "Nice guy."

Like other restaurants in this book, nearly everything served at the Parthenon was made in-house. The desserts, the yogurt, the gyros, the phyllo, you name it. Everything, that is, but the Greek bread, which was a special recipe made specifically for the Parthenon by Turano in Berwyn. Many of the ingredients in chef Stasinos's kitchen were imported from Greece, including cheeses, olives, olive oil, oregano, and most of the other herbs and spices. Typically humble to a fault, Chris was not shy when boasting about the quality of his restaurant's ingredients. "We buy expensive," he said with a knowing laugh. Clearly, this man knew what brought customers back to his restaurant time and time again. When it came to the food, the Parthenon was not willing to cut any corners.

A Long Way from Megalopoli

After he ensured that the Parthenon's kitchen was in good hands, head chef Gailas returned to Greece in the early 1980s. Most Greeks who came to America during the height of immigration planned on returning after they made some money. But that's not quite how things worked out. As more opportunities grew in the United States, the majority of Greeks stayed, making American cities like Chicago their permanent homes. In fact, about 70 percent of Greek immigrants who planned on returning to their homeland stayed in America. Greeks established ice cream shops, candy stores, confectionaries, and restaurants more than any other ethnic group in Chicago (Mourtoupalas 2014).

The Liakouras family is from Megalopoli, a city in Arcadia in the Peloponnese region. The family had a hardware store there, where Chris, his brothers Bill and George, and two cousins all worked. There wasn't enough business to support everyone, so Chris came to America in 1955 with his father, Panagiotis, and brother Bill in search of better opportunities. (His mother, Yannoula, came to America a few years later; sister Chrisoula stayed in Greece.) Chris's older brother George was supposed to make the trip, but he was drafted into the Greek army. Chris's draft papers were delayed, so in a twist of fate, he went to America instead.

Arriving in Detroit, Chris joined the U.S. Army, where he met his lifelong friend, Petros Tzafaroglou. He voluntarily served from 1956 to 1958, doing what was called "pushing the draft," or not waiting until the age of twenty-one, when young men were usually drafted. After serving a tour in Korea, his duty back in the states entailed transporting prisoners by train from Fort Harrison in Indianapolis to Detroit or, for more serious offenders, to Fort Leavenworth.

Even as a young PFC, Chris showed signs of his generous nature and gift for dealing with people. One day he was transporting a prisoner to Detroit. A nice guy, Chris remembered. Reasonable. Not dangerous. When they got to Detroit, he uncuffed his mild-mannered charge and took him to a bar, where they met up with Petros, who had been discharged a few months earlier. The three bonded over many beers. Chris turned to the prisoner and asked, "You got a girl in Detroit?" The young man replied, "Yes, sir, I do." Chris instructed him to call up his girl and "spend a wonderful night with her, because you're going to be in [prison] for a very long time. Meet me and Petros outside this bar at 7:00 in the morning. And if you don't meet me at 7:00 in the morning, I'm going to be in trouble, but you're going to be in worse trouble. Trust me. 7:00 in the morning." So he said, "Yes sir," called his girlfriend, spent the night with her, and was waiting outside the next morning—an hour early. Chris dutifully took him in.

In 1958, out of the Army and without jobs, Chris and Petros plotted their next move. Petros had a 1957 Ford Galaxy, but he was behind in payments. California was out: not enough money for gas. With $64 between them, they drove the Ford to Chicago, only 280 miles away. Both delivered the Red Book, an earlier version of the Yellow Pages, making a combined $12 a day. They lived on canned sardines and loaves of bread and rented a house on the South Side for $10 a week.

Eager to make more money, the two friends started working in a restaurant, Chris as a busboy, Petros a dishwasher. "I wasn't crazy about it," said the enterprising Chris. So he left and went to work as a chrome plater at International Harvester, a refrigerator and farm equipment manufacturer in Chicago. By that time, Petros's creditors caught up with him and impounded his car. Unaware of his misfortune, Petros walked up to an identical-looking Ford Galaxy parked nearby and unsuccessfully tried to force it open. Chris looked in the backseat and saw a baby's crib. "Petros," he said, tapping on his friend's shoulder, "you don't have any babies. That's not your car!" Undeterred, Petros called the police to report his car stolen. No one stole your car, he was told. The car was where it belonged—General Financing Detroit.

Disenchanted by factory work, Chris found a job through his father waiting tables at Mandis Chicken King, owned by another native Greek, William Mandis, at 4353 North Central Avenue on Chicago's Northwest Side. As Chris made more money and got more settled in his new city, his brother Bill joined him and Petros in their South Side apartment. The Liakouras brothers waited tables at Mandis Chicken King six days a week, fourteen hours a day, making over $1,000 a week—about $400,000 a year by 2018 standards. At Mandis, Chris learned how to perch multiple plates of food on each arm, a tradition carried on by Greek restaurants. One day, he was balancing over a dozen bowls of soup on his arms when he collided with a busboy on the other side of a swinging kitchen door. The bowls crashed to the floor, the hot broth splashing all over him. Mandis's manager started screaming, angry about the huge mess. Chris fired back some well-chosen words picked up in the Army, tossed his apron on the floor, and quit.

He quickly landed another job waiting tables at Diana's Grocery and Restaurant at 310 South Halsted. Like many Greek eateries at the time, Diana's had a grocery store in front, dining room in back. Bill left Mandis Chicken King shortly afterward and joined his brother at Diana's. The two worked long hours, pooling their hard-earned tips in the hope of opening their own place. About three years later, the brothers found out that the restaurant next door, Gyros, was going out of business. They wandered over, talked to the owner, and struck a deal over a bottle of retsina to purchase Gyros for $38,000. They changed the restaurant's name to the Parthenon, and an institution was born. Chris worked the floor, with Bill behind the bar and Gyros's chef, Gailas, in the kitchen.

Opening Day

On their first day of business (July 5, 1968, also Chris's birthday), they made a modest $110. Two months later, they had a line waiting out the door for one of the ninety seats. Made-to-order gyros and flaming saganaki were a hit. After about ten months of steadily growing business, thieves broke into the restaurant's safe and stole $14,000—a huge chunk of their savings. Chris was sure, even forty-eight years later, that it was an inside job. Someone who knew the routine at the restaurant, where the money was. The next day all of Chicago's media came out. "They were here about the 'Robbery at the Parthenon!'" said Chris. It was the Liakouras's first brush with fame. "My brother was really worried," Chris remembered. "I said, 'Listen. What are you worried about? We just got $200,000 worth of advertising!'" he said, laughing, taking things in his usual what-are-you-gonna-do stride.

After the media blitz, business skyrocketed. The Parthenon's food was soon featured in the *Chicago Tribune*, *Chicago Sun-Times*, *Daily News*, *Chicago Guide* (now *Chicago* magazine), and the *New York Times*. In 1973, the Liakouras brothers bought the space next door at 316 South Halsted and expanded by about 175 seats. Those were the Parthenon's halcyon days. Dr. Randy Pachnik, who was a regular at the restaurant and there on opening day, remembered them well. "Friday and Saturday nights, it was ridiculous," he said one day while having lunch at the bar, the summer before it closed. "There would be lines out the door. They'd bring out the ouzo. And not just one time. By the time people got to the door, they were already well lubricated."

Chicago's Greektown started to shape into what it is today. A Greek pharmacy appeared on Halsted. Pan Hellenic Pastry Shop opened in 1974 at 322 South Halsted. A Greek grocery appeared. In 1961 Athenian Candle Company, which has been in business since 1922, moved to its current location at 300 South Halsted.

As Greektown began to flourish and word spread about the Parthenon's famous flaming saganaki, gyros, and other traditional Greek favorites, celebrities and local politicians began to pour in. "Who didn't come here?" Chris responded when asked to name names. In the late 1960s and early 1970s, Mayor Richard J. Daley used to send his driver in to the restaurant to cash what Chris assumed was the Mayor's paycheck. "I figured out that at that time he was making about $75,000 a year," said Chris. "They wanted cash. They didn't want to put it in the bank."

The restaurant's walls were covered with photos of some of the celebs who passed through the Parthenon's doors in those days, including Jane Russell, Dom DeLuise, and actress Joey Heatherton. One day, a customer asked a server to turn down the music so that he could hear his dinner conversation. The server took the complaint to Bill, who instructed him to tell the customer he was sorry, but that the volume could not be turned up or down. Chris recognized the customer, and grabbed the waiter to ask him what was going on. The server explained. Chris rushed over to his brother. "Do you know who that guy is?" No, said Bill. "That's Marcello Mastroianni!" Chris cried. "He turns the music down anytime he wants!"

Besides "old man Daley," Governors George Ryan and Rod Blagojevich both used to come in on a regular basis. Everyone crossed paths with the Parthenon, said Chris, from Chicago Mayor Rahm Emanuel to Democrats, Republicans, the Blackhawks, the Bulls, local news anchors, teacher's union reps, and all walks of life in between. "You ask anybody in Chicago," laughed Chris, "they've been in Parthenon at least once."

Greektown Revitalization Project

After the Parthenon opened, more Greek restaurants appeared on Halsted Street, including Greek Islands in 1971, Rodity's in 1973, and Santorini's in 1987, with Pegasus, Athena, Artopolis, and 9 Muses following in the 1990s (Pegasus closed in December 2017). The restaurant business on Halsted Street boomed from the '70s through the '90s, said Chris, but diners were ushered in and out of their cars by the valets. They weren't exploring the neighborhood. The surrounding area, which includes the Near West Side and West Loop, was in steep decline. Step one block west of Halsted and there was a large population of panhandlers looking for a quarter or a drink. All the Greektown restaurants had parking attendants out front, so they were the only ones really dealing with it, not the customers. Chris's daughter

Yanna, who as a kid checked coats and washed glasses behind the restaurant's bar until a cop kicked her out for being underage, recalled that "No one was dangerous. They were just looking for a handout."

Greek-owned businesses were pushed to the small stretch of Halsted between Van Buren and Monroe after Chicago's original Greektown was demolished in the 1960s to make way for the UIC campus and new expressways. The overall population of the Near West Side diminished by approximately one-third between 1970 and 1985 (Louik/Schneider & Associates 1996).

The Near West Side was once a strong manufacturing and industrial district. In the mid-1970s, the City of Chicago designated a portion of the West Side dubbed Madison-Racine "slum and blight." By 1980, the city redesignated this area as a "blighted commercial area." Many factors were to blame: the construction of the Dan Ryan Expressway, low-income residents moving to the area, and changing retail habits. Many buildings were older and run-down (Louik/Schneider & Associates 1996).

The city saw an urgent need to stimulate economic activity on the Near West Side as well as strengthen Greektown's identity. In 1996, the United Hellenic American Congress and the city launched a major revitalization project for the area, which received a push when Chicago was chosen to host the 1996 Democratic National Convention at the United Center. The president of Greece, Costis Stephanopoulis, His Eminence Metropolitan Iakovos, and Mayor Richard M. Daley commenced the project at a ceremony in May 1996. The multimillion-dollar plan included new streetscapes and two templelike structures on Halsted at Monroe and Van Buren to mark the northern and southern borders of Greektown, respectively. Three forty-five-foot Grecian pillars, each representing a different age of civilization, stand at the Adams, Quincy, and Monroe access ramps to the Kennedy Expressway, visible far and wide (Ganakos 2005).

Greektown's revitalization was firmly entrenched when the National Hellenic Museum moved to its new 40,000-square foot location at 333 South Halsted in December 2011. The museum is home to extensive archives and collections spanning thousands of years. Its main focus is to preserve the Greek immigration experience through oral histories, photography, and other documentation. The modern, four-story museum's rooftop terrace offers sweeping views of the city. It is the crown jewel of Chicago's modern-day Greektown.

The Second Generation

By the time Yanna Liakouras came back to work at the Parthenon as an adult in 1995, Chicago's Greektown was safer and more established than it was in the 1970s. Yanna never entertained the idea of staying in Chicago and working at her father's restaurant. After high school, she attended Loyola University, got married, moved to California, and worked in the banking industry. After her divorce, Yanna's father asked her to move back to Chicago and join the Parthenon family in 1995. She became partner shortly after.

Like his sister, Peter Liakouras didn't plan on a career in the family business, either. He joined the U.S. Army after high school and worked as a server at the Parthenon on and off before joining the full-time staff in 1999. He managed the dinner shift, a post he held for more than fifteen years until the restaurant closed. Like his sister and father, Peter always greeted customers with a gracious warmth, staying on top of the mountain of details that confront restaurant staff on any given day.

During the Parthenon's last years, Yanna would station herself at the restaurant's entrance after her father left for the day. She almost never sat still during her shift, either answering the restaurant's phone, which rang off the hook, greeting the regular stream of customers, or checking her cell phone, which sprang to life with the theme to *The Godfather* as its ringtone. Yanna said she learned everything from her father. The only woman in a staff of about fifty, the biggest lesson she's learned, she said, is that no matter how complicated a situation is, deal with it immediately and deal with it the simplest way you know how.

"Maybe women tend to overcomplicate things, you know what I mean?" she said, treading lightly on a topic that she realized could offend her own sex. "I've been in the male environment so many years, I don't do that. As a matter of fact, I've learned a lesson about myself. Your biggest saboteur is your brain. And when it starts sabotaging you, because it can sabotage you, the best thing to do is stop."

Besides her father's no-nonsense approach to life in general, Yanna also inherited his gracious personality. As she flitted about the restaurant like a pinball machine, attending to all matters at hand, she did so with a congenial ease, making customers feel like honored guests in her home. The embodiment of *filoxenia*.

The Burgeoning West Loop

Back in the 1990s, Chicago's business landscape was much different than it is today. Although the Parthenon's lunch business was still going strong in 2016, it was nothing like it was in the 1980s and 1990s, when diners splurged on cocktail-heavy business lunches and charged them to company expense accounts. Eventually, businesses tightened their belts and started frowning on drinking during work events, citing liability issues. There is also much more competition. The Loop is now filled with restaurants. People can just walk from their office to the closest restaurant, as opposed to taking a cab to Greektown.

Businesses have also moved out of the downtown area and relocated to the suburbs to avoid higher taxes. The congestion on the Kennedy is also a factor. Yanna said it used to take her father ten minutes to get from his home in Norridge to the restaurant. "No one wants to spend two hours on the Kennedy to go out to eat." To avoid lengthy commutes, Chris and his second wife, Lorraine, moved to the top floor of the Parthenon's building, and Yanna moved into the apartment below, where she lived until the Parthenon closed.

The West Loop, Fulton Market, and Fulton River District neighborhoods started experiencing a tremendous boom in residential and commercial development around 2015. Restaurants, retailers, and business giants like Google moved into the area, which offers proximity to downtown. Real estate values have skyrocketed for some commercial properties in Greektown (Ori 2015). But the recent surge to the area hasn't necessarily translated to a surge in business. Newcomers are young, and they have high mortgages, said Yanna. They can't spend as much money as workers could in the '80s or '90s. "It's not a matter of how many people you have, it's also a matter of how much money those people have to spend," she stated. "Things have changed over the years. People stick to their own neighborhoods now."

Her father echoed Yanna's assessment. "Things are not as great as they used to be, you know. Generally, the businesses are down," he said, referring to other businesses in Greektown and the lingering effects of the most recent recession. "They're not the way they used to be in the '70s, '80s, '90s. Right now, it's a little bit different."

Things are not bleak, just changed. Greektown's restaurants continue to attract the same Greek families who have been coming to this neighborhood for decades. In fact, throughout its entire history, all of the Parthenon's staff members—no matter their native language—were required to learn Greek to accommodate the 20 percent or so of customers whose first language was Greek. Salvador Martinez, who worked at the Parthenon from 1980 to 2016, served three generations of several Greek families. The same customers who once sat in a high chair, he said, came in with their children to celebrate birthdays, engagements, weddings, anniversaries, graduations—all of life's main events.

Greektown is still a popular destination for business lunches and dinners, despite the decline since the more decadent '80s and '90s. Many local organizations meet here, as well as McCormick Place convention attendees from all over the world. Chris's wife, Lorraine Rieff Liakouras, a successful businessperson throughout her career, opened Chicago Parthenon Guest House on the three upper floors at 310 South Halsted. The hostel, which opened in 2010, attracts tourists from all over the world.

As any business owner knows, recruiting and retaining good employees is one of the hardest aspects of business. Restaurants suffer from higher-than-average turnover rates, as many employees are students or work part-time. The Parthenon, it seems, didn't get this memo. In fact, the restaurant enjoyed an employee retention rate that any Fortune 500 corporation would envy. Martinez, whom staff affectionately referred to as "Pueblo," served flaming saganaki at the Parthenon for thirty-six years. His tenure is bested by Markos Lekas, another server who was with the Liakouras family since the 1970s. Bartender Manuel Gonzalez, who started as a busboy, also worked at the Parthenon from the 1970s until it closed. Stasinos, of course, was head chef, perfecting time-honored recipes from 1976 until 2016. Chris estimated that most of the waiters and cooks had an average tenure of fifteen years. Some of the valets had been there for ten years or more.

When a staff member did leave, there was always a cousin or a brother waiting to take his place. In 2015, Yanna placed a Craigslist ad for a dishwasher and a part-time cleaning service. It was the only time in her career at the Parthenon she ever had to advertise for help.

One afternoon, as Chris and I sat talking at the Parthenon's bar near the front entrance, yet another plume of flaming saganaki was served at a table nearby. The customers' eyes lit up as everyone joined the server with an exuberant "Opaa!" Even this city cynic doesn't tire of that scene. People did come to the Parthenon for the food. But they came back for the *filoxenia*.

Kali Orexi!
Greek for *bon appetit!*

Isigian!
Greek equivalent of "cheers!"

Spanakotyropita (Spinach-cheese pies)

This was my favorite dish at the Parthenon. I always ordered the entrée, but it was also served as an appetizer. If you prefer less spinach, use 4 lbs. or less, to suit your tastes. If you use frozen phyllo, make sure you allow several hours for it to defrost.

Ingredients

1 lb. phyllo leaves, 12 × 15 inches
5 lbs. fresh spinach, coarsely
   chopped, or 8 10-oz. packages
   frozen chopped spinach, thawed
¾ c. olive oil
About ½ c. finely chopped green
   onions (5–6)

¼ c. (4 oz.) finely chopped
   fresh dill
½ tsp. ground black pepper
2 large eggs
2 lbs. Greek feta cheese,
   crumbled
½ c. (¼ lb.) butter, melted

Directions

1. *Allow phyllo leaves to warm to room temperature, according to package directions.*

2. *Preheat oven to 350° F.*

3. *If using fresh spinach*: Wash very well in several rinses of fresh water. Add the spinach to a large pan, cover, and place over low heat, simmering until spinach wilts (about 10 minutes), stirring occasionally. Drain spinach. (It is recommended to rinse spinach several times to remove dirt, sand, bugs, etc.) *If using frozen spinach*: Drain thawed spinach well, squeezing out liquid.

4. Add oil to a large skillet and place over medium heat. When oil is hot, sauté the onions until they begin to sizzle. Add the dill and stir. Add the

drained spinach and the pepper and stir over medium heat for about 15 minutes. Remove skillet from heat.

5. In small bowl, beat the 2 eggs and add to the skillet. Add the feta cheese and mix well.

6. Brush a 9 × 13 × 2-inch baking pan lightly with some of the melted butter. Place a leaf of phyllo in bottom of baking pan, so half of the leaf is in the pan and the other half hangs over edge of the pan. Brush top of phyllo leaf with melted butter. Repeat procedure for 4 to 5 layers of phyllo. While working, keep unused phyllo leaves covered with damp paper towels to prevent them from drying out.

7. Spread spinach mixture evenly over phyllo in pan. Cover the spinach-cheese mixture with the portion of phyllo that is hanging over the edge of the pan. Place another 4 leaves of phyllo on top while brushing each leaf with melted butter. Without cutting all the way through, use a sharp knife to cut the top layer on a diagonal; then cut in opposite direction to form about 9 3-inch diamonds.

8. Bake in preheated oven for 30 to 35 minutes, or until the top crust is puffy and golden. Serve hot.

Makes six to nine appetizer servings.

Saganaki

No trip to the Parthenon was complete without an order of saganaki. In its forty-eight years in business, only one server—the only female server ever hired at the Parthenon—lit her hair on fire while serving the restaurant's famous flaming dish.

Ingredients

½ c. milk
1 egg
1 lb. kasseri cheese, sliced ½-inch thick
1 c. flour

Vegetable oil, as needed
2 lemons, halved
Greek bread

Directions

1. Beat milk and egg together (batter is sufficient for 4 or 5 slices of cheese).

2. Dip each cheese slice in milk mixture and then in flour. Shake off excess flour. Refrigerate 1 to 3 hours.

3. Pour about ¼ inch of oil in frying pan. Heat oil over medium-low heat, making sure the oil is not too hot. Brown slices in hot oil, about 1 minute per side. Remove and place on heated metal steak plates or individual frying pans. Squeeze lemon juice over the cheese. Serve hot with Greek bread.

Five

BORINQUEN
Home of the Jibaro

If you live in Chicago, you might think that the jibarito—*a sandwich served at Puerto Rican restaurants throughout the city—is a staple in Puerto Rican food. But you probably won't find it anywhere in Puerto Rico. It was invented in Chicago by Peter Figueroa in 1990. Though his family's restaurant, Borinquen, is now closed, Peter's legendary sandwich has become a permanent fixture throughout Chicago.*

I first met Peter Figueroa, a Chicago transplant from Jayuya, Puerto Rico, on a hot summer afternoon in 2007 at his restaurant, Borinquen, at 1720 North California Avenue in Chicago's Humboldt Park neighborhood. Business was skyrocketing. Though it was between lunch and dinner, a line of customers snaked around Borinquen's ninety-seat space and out the door. Every inch of the place was packed with customers, mostly families, loading up on jibarito sandwiches, Peter's invention and claim to fame.* Staff wove in and out of

---

*Peter Figueroa is from Jayuya, which features one of the highest mountain ranges in Puerto Rico. After he created his famous sandwich, he and his father brainstormed and came up with a name for it: the *jibarito*, the diminutive of the word *jibaro*. Though

the thick crowd. Think Hot Doug's, with Puerto Rican food instead of artisanal sausages. In the midst of the chaos, Peter looked exhausted, but happy.

"We used to have . . . one-hundred people waiting in line outside my restaurant," said Peter. "It was a madhouse. At one point, we were buying twenty cases of fifty pounds [of plantains] a day. On a given day we could make 1,000 jibaritos." Jibarito: the sandwich that put Figueroa—and Borinquen—on the map. ("Borinquen" is the word given to Puerto Rico by its original inhabitants, the Taíno Indians.) Unlike other claims made about various foods in Chicago, there seems to be no dispute that Peter Figueroa invented the jibarito, the word a diminutive of *jibaro*, itself an affectionate term for someone from the mountains of Puerto Rico.

The Birth of the Jibarito

Peter created his famous sandwich in 1990. He was at Borinquen reading *El Vocero*, a Puerto Rican newspaper distributed in Chicago. "Every day, when I went to the store to buy my supplies, I would grab the newspaper," said Peter, who bounces between English and Spanish in a thick Puerto Rican accent. "The first thing I would always read was the recipes." It was in *El Vocero* that Peter found the recipe for the *sandwich de plátano*, or plantain sandwich. "It was basically a steak sandwich," said Peter, always comfortable in storytelling mode. But instead of bread, the steak was housed between two slabs of fried green plantain, a starchier cousin of the sweet banana that Americans gobble up by the ton every year.

Peter made the *sandwich de plátano*, adding his own lettuce, tomatoes, mayo, American cheese, and a smear of fresh, smashed garlic. "I Americanized it," he said. "I made one for my father. He went bananas," Peter continued, so caught up in the retelling of his oft-told tale that he missed his obvious pun. "He went crazy. He said, 'Peter, this is what we've been looking for. This is gonna make us rich.'"

---

it has no direct English translation, *jibaro* is commonly compared to "hillbilly." It's an affectionate term for someone who lives in the mountains. Said Peter of his famous creation: "It's a sandwich for the people from the mountains, the *jibaro*."

"Papa Juan's" words proved prophetic as word spread about the decadent steak sandwich served in Humboldt Park. "I started giving it to people, making it for my friends, promoting it at the restaurant," said Peter. "All of the sudden, we have a full house." The American-ized version of the *sandwich de plátano* was born. Borinquen became known as "home of the *jibaro*."

"The most famous one was made with steak," said Peter. "We used to cut the beef real thin . . . added oil and adobo, adobo is a dry sea-soning, and then put a lot of onion in that and let it boil. Then we start slicing plantains, deep-fry 'em. When they float, they're ready to smash. We smash 'em, then we deep fry them again to make 'em crispy. We started with steak. But all of a sudden, people said, 'Can you make mine with chicken?' Skin and legs. Deep fried. With 'skin and all.' The skin gets real nice and crispy, and then when you bite, it kind of cracks." During its nearly three-decade run across three differ-ent locations, Borinquen made nine varieties of the jibarito, including a breakfast sandwich called the "breakfast jib."*

The jibarito helped catapult Borinquen's business throughout the 1990s (it opened in 1987). In 2000, the restaurant got another major break when reporter Monica Eng gave it a glowing review in the *Chicago Tribune*. "My grandmother was a great Puerto Rican cook," said Eng in a phone interview. "She was the one who recommended the place." Eng featured the jibarito in another *Tribune* article in 2003, calling it a "Midwestern delicacy: a Chicago sandwich, albeit with island roots." Said Eng, "The jibarito was quite a sensation. Like I said in my story, even Mexican restaurants were making it. It's at Taste of Chicago now."

Riding this wave of success, in 2001 Peter opened a second Borin-quen on the Northwest Side at 3020 North Central, with his brother

---

*The first Borinquen Restaurant at 1720 North California was open from 1987 to 2012. A second location at 3020 North Central was open from 2001 to 2013. A third and fi-nal location at 5247 West Belmont operated from 2013 to 2016. Borinquen Lounge on Western Avenue was originally a nightclub operated by one of Peter's brothers. Peter's nephew Eric runs Borinquen Lounge as a restaurant and bar; it carries traditional Puer-to Rican food and the *jibarito*. Peter's father, siblings, in-laws, and friends have been involved in Borinquen's businesses intermittently over the years, taking over entirely when Peter left the business in 2007.

Fernando in charge. Peter continued to manage the California location and served as the restaurant's spokesperson. The family business was in full swing. By 2007, Peter and the jibarito had been covered by the *Chicago Reader*, *Chicago's Best*, *Not For Tourists Guide to Chicago*, the *Chicago Sun-Times*, *Time Out Chicago*, ABC 7's "Hungry Hound," and others. *Esquire* magazine added the jibarito to its "best sandwiches in America" list. A *Chicago Tribune* article revised fifteen of the entries in Patricia Schultz's book, *Places to See in Chicago before You Die*, replacing Schultz's pick of Arun's with Borinquen: "Birthplace of the *jibaro*, a Puerto Rican-style sandwich" (*Chicago Tribune* 2007).

Peter became a media pro. Lines for jibaritos continued to form at the California and Central locations. By all appearances, 2007 was the height of Borinquen's success. It was also the year that Peter left the business.

Feasts on a *Fogón*

The Figueroa family is from Jayuya, Puerto Rico. "I'm from the mountains," said Peter, "four thousand feet up." He's known as Peter, though his real name is Juan Carlos. When his mother was pregnant, he said, "she was listening to a soap opera on the radio. There was no TV then. The main character, his name was Juan Carlos Santa Cruz. He was . . . very famous. So she said that she was going to call me Juan Carlos."

It was Peter's maternal grandmother who exposed him to traditional Puerto Rican cooking. "When we were living in San Juan . . . I would say to my mom, 'Can I go over to Grandma's for a few days?' My grandfather had died, so I wanted to keep her company. It was only her and me. For breakfast, she would cook ten or fifteen different things and put them on the table for me. She would do fried eggs, and boiled eggs, she would do ham, *bacalaitos*, canned sausage, sweet plantains, tostones . . ." Peter found out that his grandma also fed any stranger who knocked on her door looking for food. "With my grandma, it was always rice and beans and a pork chop. And you better eat the pork chop first. While you're eating, if a visitor comes, they take the meat away from you!" he said laughing.

What is perhaps most notable about these multicourse Puerto Rican feasts is that "mama" cooked them on a *fogón*, a simple wood-burning stove. A *fogón*, Peter explained, was "a box the size of a stove with dirt . . . and four rocks." She would place firewood in the *fogón* with the rocks, light it, and cook her favorites. "My mom had one, too," he said. Mama didn't let Peter cook. "I would just look. I watched." But these experiences had a profound influence on him. "When I cook, I cook the style that my grandmother did."

Chicago's Puerto Rican Community

The United States acquired Puerto Rico after the Spanish-American War of 1898. The Jones Act, which was enacted by Congress in 1917, granted all Puerto Ricans U.S. citizenship. But the first major wave of Puerto Rican migration did not occur until after World War II, with the vast majority moving to New York. As of 2012, New York still boasted the largest Puerto Rican population in the country—six times that of Chicagoland's (Cintrón et al. 2012).

Puerto Ricans who first came to Chicago settled in various neighborhoods, including the Near North Side, which suffered from neglect in the 1940s and 1950s as whites fled for the suburbs, leaving behind deteriorating buildings, crowded living conditions, and cheaper rent. A Puerto Rican enclave centered at LaSalle and Superior was displaced in the late 1960s when Arthur Rubloff landed a deal to develop the area. The project, named Carl Sandburg Village, was completed in 1971 and displaced approximately 900 families (Fernandez 2012, 132–41).

Some of these displaced Puerto Rican families moved from their Near North homes to Cabrini Green's low-rise and high-rise apartments. In historian Lilia Fernandez's book *Brown in the Windy City*, Cabrini-Green resident Monse Lucas-Figueroa recalled how the buildings in the projects were unofficially divided by race: "from the first to seventh floor were *familias Latinas*. From the seventh floor to the tenth floor belonged to the *blanquitos*, the hillbilly families. From there on up were all black families. That's why all the fights started!" (Fernandez 2012, 144–45).

To acknowledge Chicago's growing Puerto Rican community, in 1966 Mayor Richard J. Daley designated the first week in June as Puerto Rican Week. Thousands gathered along State Street for the city's first

Puerto Rican parade on June 12, 1966. A post-parade gathering near Damen and Division, however, became violent after a teenage boy was shot in the leg by police. The Division Street Riots ensued for three days. According to a *Chicago Sun-Times* article published that week, there were sixteen injured, forty-nine arrested, about fifty buildings destroyed, and two police cars burned (*Chicago Sun-Times* 1966). The event brought awareness to the social and economic challenges that Puerto Ricans faced in Chicago. The fiftieth anniversary of the riots was commemorated at the Puerto Rican People's Parade in June 2016 to honor this significant chapter in Chicago's history.

Chicago's Lincoln Park neighborhood was also considered a slum during the postwar period. Developers identified the valuable lakefront community for urban renewal projects in the late 1960s. Housing prices subsequently soared, forcing many low-income families to move. "Following their displacement from Lincoln Park," wrote Wilfredo Cruz in *Puerto Rican Chicago*, "most Puerto Ricans moved west to Division Street to West Town, Bucktown, and Wicker Park" (Cruz 2004, 31). In the period 1960–80, West Town and Humboldt Park became known as Puerto Rican barrios (Fernandez 2012, 152).

Peter's father came to the United States in the late 1960s, moving first to New York before settling in Chicago near Barry and Clark. His eldest sons followed. Peter arrived in Chicago in 1976, when the family was living in Bucktown near Western and Dickens. "Little by little, we moved around the city," said Peter, describing a migration pattern common to the entire Puerto Rican community. But Bucktown, said Peter, was the first neighborhood that he encountered in Chicago.

Papa Juan's Influence

A framed photograph of Papa Juan hamming it up on a motorcycle was prominently displayed at the last Borinquen location on Belmont, which closed in the summer of 2016. One day, when I came to meet Peter, he was sitting near the photo, silently praying to it as though to a sacred shrine. "My father, he was my mentor. He was my best friend." In 2002, fifteen years after the Figueroas finally struck restaurant gold at 1720 North California, the place that local radio personality Rey Rubio coined "La Casa del *Jibaro*," Papa Juan passed away. "He always believed in me," said Peter. "He was like an amazing man, you know? He was not a cook. But he gave me so many ideas."

Peter experienced what can only be described as an incredibly successful twenty-year run at Borinquen before he left the business in 2007, citing burnout and financial woes. But it was only after a long string of short-term successes and failures that he finally hit the jackpot with Borinquen. A serial entrepreneur at heart, Peter was involved with several other ventures in both Chicago and Puerto Rico, usually with various family members, including his father. If it was his maternal grandmother who influenced him as a cook, it was his father who encouraged Peter's creativity and entrepreneurial side.

"One time he came by," Peter said of his father, "and he gave me five thousand dollars. He told me, 'Let's open up a restaurant.' And we opened it, and we failed, and we opened another one, and it failed. He helped me every time I failed."

Peter and Papa Juan's first venture was a social club in Humboldt Park called Cabaña. Opened in the late 1970s, the club had a little kitchen in the back, where Peter first started to cook. When Cabaña folded, Peter and his father opened a liquor and convenience store called Figueroa Food & Liquor at Western and McLean, where they sold groceries, booze, and homemade Puerto Rican food "through a little window." At the same time the family also ran El Flamboyán, also in West Bucktown.

After Figueroa Food & Liquor closed, frustrated and tired, Peter decided to go back to Puerto Rico, where his mother still lived (his parents separated in 1967). He cooked on the line at a Cuban restaurant, where all he did was "make *mofongo*. Just *mofongo*." He decided to return to the better economic climate in Chicago, working at El Parador at Division and Hoyne with Papa Juan, his brother Angel, and a friend. They served American fast food. Slowly, they started offering Puerto Rican food like Peter's now-mastered *mofongo* and *alcapurrias*. Customers who had grown in love with Peter's homemade Puerto Rican cooking at Figueroa Food & Liquor started coming around. "A lot of people followed me from that little store I had," said Peter. "They followed me to Division Street and Hoyne. I could only seat about fifteen people, and sometimes I had twenty or thirty people outside. That's even before the jibarito."

Peter noticed that a growing number of El Parador's deliveries were to Chicago's Northwest Side. "A lot of Puerto Ricans started moving out there," said Peter, "so I told my brother Fernando, 'We should open a place out there.'" Peter's final venture before Borinquen was Isleno Restaurant, a sit-down eatery opened in the mid-1980s near Pulaski and North. "That's when most people started moving to the Northwest Side."

Paseo Boricua

The Paseo Boricua (Puerto Rican public square), located on Division Street between Western and California in Humboldt Park, is Chicago's official Puerto Rican commercial district. Mayor Richard M. Daley inaugurated the Paseo Boricua on January 6, 1995, the same day that the Puerto Rican community celebrates Dia de Los Reyes, or Three Kings Day. Two forty-five-ton steel Puerto Rican flags wave from the eastern and western portals of Paseo Boricua. The intentions of these fifty-nine-foot, looming structures, part of the city's $2.5 million beautification project, seem overbearing once you take a stroll down this lazy half-mile stretch.

There are about half dozen or so Puerto Rican restaurants on the Paseo Boricua, inviting customers in for *sancocho* or a jibarito with a mouthwatering waft of garlic, each translating Puerto Rican food in its own way. On a typical afternoon, the Paseo is mostly quiet, save for the music coming out of Lily's Record Shop, which has carried a world-class salsa selection since 1983. A slew of medical offices and storefront places of worship offer healing in its various forms. On a warm day, a group of men usually gather on the sidewalk in front of Jayuya Barber to play dominoes. There are more barbershops than bars. A large number of social service agencies dot the landscape. A couple of bakeries and cafes beckon. A florist, a grocery, a Chinese takeout joint—essential in any neighborhood—and a couple of liquor stores, at the most, reside on this strip.

The Puerto Rican flag is omnipresent on Paseo Boricua, waving from apartment balconies and prominent on murals splashed on buildings, depicting the people and places of Puerto Rico in the vivid colors of the Caribbean. Political signs and posters are a common sight in storefront windows. By all accounts, Paseo Boricua caters to the neighborhood's past and present residents looking for an authentic Puerto Rican meal, not flocks of tourists hunting for souvenirs.

A noticeable number of storefronts are vacant.

The City of Chicago's Puerto Rican population was once concentrated in the area surrounding Paseo Boricua. According to the U.S. Census and local business owners, however, this is no longer the case. The Puerto Rican population started to disperse in the 1990s, building communities in neighborhoods such as Hermosa, Cragin, and Logan Square, all on Chicago's Northwest Side (Cintrón 2012).

"There's not that many Puerto Ricans in Humboldt Park anymore," said Jaime Cruz, third-generation owner of Latin American Restaurant & Lounge at 2743 West Division, in business since 1958. "It was too late," said Cruz of the city's designation of the Paseo Boricua in 1995. "There weren't as many Puerto Ricans in Humboldt Park" in the 1990s as in the 1980s. Now, he said, "all types of ethnicities" live in Humboldt Park. "A lot of Puerto Ricans retired to Florida and Puerto Rico," said Cruz. "They sold for profit."

Since 2000, however, Puerto Ricans have been migrating to the United States in the largest numbers since the postwar Great Migration. There have been more Puerto Ricans living on the mainland than the island since at least 2006 (Cohn, Patten, and Lopez 2014). But Chicago doesn't seem to be a destination for this new wave. Though the city of Chicago continues to boast a large Puerto Rican community—the third most populous in the United States, after New York and Philadelphia—population growth in Chicago has stagnated. Recent migrants are mostly moving to cities in Florida (Cintrón 2012).

The Ubiquitous Jibarito

Borinquen on California closed in 2012. A new Puerto Rican restaurant has since moved in, named El Nuevo Borinquen, unrelated to the Figueroa family. I asked Peter whether it bothered him that they are using a name so similar to his, or that the jibarito, his creation, is now served by restaurants throughout the city. No, he said, it doesn't bother him at all. Peter seems much more concerned about the level of quality at which his invention is reproduced, not the credit. "A lot of people are duplicating my sandwich, but I'm flattered. Hey, if they make money, and they do things right, and represent me well, I'm happy, you know?"

Peter's legacy is firmly entrenched in Chicago, evident by what can only be described as the ubiquitous nature of the jibarito, now over a quarter-century old. It is evident at Division and California, the southeast corner of Humboldt Park, where park district concession stands named "*El Jibarito* Place" hawk jibaritos and other Puerto Rican food. It is evident on Paseo Boricua, where the jibarito is featured on every Puerto Rican menu.

It is evident in Latin restaurants around the city. Restaurants like La Bomba, a family-owned Puerto Rican restaurant in Logan Square, which served full and tasting portions of the jibarito at the 2016 Taste of Chicago. Puerto Rican, Cuban, and Mexican restaurants throughout Humboldt Park, Logan Square, Little Village, and Pilsen all serve the jibarito, tipping their hat to Peter as its famous creator. Jaime Cruz is one of them. "He was the inventor," said Cruz of Peter's claim to the jibarito. Cruz spoke highly of Figueroa as we chatted in his cramped basement office below his family's restaurant on Paseo Boricua, a figurine of *el coqui*, Puerto Rico's symbolic tree frog, resting on top of his desk. Cruz's jibaritos come with chicken, steak, or pork. Jibaritos represent "a good 30 percent" of his sales, said Cruz. "It's a very popular item."

Victor and Nancy Garcia own Papa's Cache Sobroso down the street at 2517 West Division. Papa's was originally located at 1642 North California, in the same block as the original Borinquen, before moving to Division in 2002. Victor confirmed that Peter Figueroa invented the sandwich, albeit with a hint of concession. "I called Pete up, and I asked him if it was ok if I made the jibarito. He said sure!" Papa's specializes in *pollo chon*, a rotisserie chicken made with a proprietary marinade. Combined receipts from the *pollo chon* and jibaritos are "a little more than half" of Papa's business, said Victor.

While the jibarito is considered standard on Latin menus throughout Chicago, neither Cruz nor Garcia has ever seen it in their native Puerto Rico. When I asked Peter if he's spotted his sandwich anywhere in Puerto Rico, he revealed a little-known detail in his history: it was served at the Jayuya, Puerto Rico outpost of Borinquen, which was open for about five years during the same time that the family was running the California and Central locations in Chicago. "Yes . . . I had a restaurant in Puerto Rico," said Peter. "My father kept telling me, 'Let's open up a restaurant in Puerto Rico.' We kept arguing. He tells me, 'Peter, I found a restaurant in Jayuya, and I signed a lease for five years.'" But the jibarito didn't fare nearly as well as it did in Chicago, and Borinquen in Jayuya was shuttered before its five-year lease ran out.

In all his years in business, Peter remembers only one complaint about the jibarito. It was sometime around 1995. "This lady walked in the restaurant, and she goes, 'I'm tired of eating jibaritos. I want a *jibarita!*' I didn't know what to say. So I said, 'How do I do that?' And she goes [in a very drawn out, seductive tone] '*platano maduro*' [sweet plantain]. It was hard to make, because when you cook sweet plantains, it doesn't stay hard, it's soft, so it's gotta be in like, a meal. You have to eat it with a fork and knife. And that lady, she bought ten of 'em the same day. People went crazy about it, too."

Borinquen's Menu: Classic Puerto Rican Food

Another Borinquen specialty was the *volcano relleno*, a twist on *mofongo*. For the uninitiated, *mofongo*, a popular Cuban and Puerto Rican dish, is a bit like a matzo ball, but made with fried, smashed plantains, then mixed with pig skin, garlic, salt, and oil and served in homemade chicken broth. *Volcano relleno* is *mofongo* shaped in the form of a little volcano that "erupts" with chicken broth. It was "basically the same thing" as *mofongo*, said Peter, but with a more playful presentation.

Borinquen was also known for its *sancocho*, a traditional Puerto Rican stew containing pig's feet, root vegetables, and homemade *sofrito*. Like Borinquen's other seasonings and condiments, the restaurant's *sofrito*—a dried herbal mixture used to season sauces—was made from scratch. Made with garlic, cilantro, and sweet peppers, it's used in stews, broths, and rice dishes such as *arroz con gandules*, or pigeon peas and rice, a Puerto Rican staple.

When the jibarito started to appear at other joints around the city, Borinquen added a side of *arroz con gandules* with every sandwich to remain competitive.

Borinquen's menu didn't change much over the years. The Figueroas stuck with traditional Puerto Rican fare like *bacalaitos* (fried cod fish patties), *alcapurrias* (fried dumplings with banana), *ensalada de pulpo* (octopus salad), and *pinchos* (fried chicken or pork kebabs).

And yes. Most Puerto Rican food is fried.

Though his days at Borinquen are behind him, Peter continues to experiment with recipes, perhaps for a future food truck. He mostly plays around with Caribbean food, using root vegetables and tropical fruits in various empanadas and other finger foods. His pet projects are the hamburger jibarito and sliders made with plantains, yucca, or *pana*, a breadfruit that migrated to Puerto Rico. "I also make tostones out of that," he said. He has also created his own line of salsas, including *salsa jibara*, which blends a variety of sweet and hot peppers; and *vinagre jibaro*, a wicked-hot vinegar-based condiment made with tabasco sauce, garlic, herbs, spices, and pineapple. Both are packaged with labels designed by a Puerto Rican artist and are available at a handful of businesses around Chicago, such as Armitage Produce at Armitage and Kimball.

"My biggest accomplishment in life is not the jibarito," said Peter while we chatted in Borinquen's back dining room, away from the music playing overhead. "When my uncle died in New York, they decided to sell the farm where I was born. I had told my uncle that if he ever wanted to sell it, and I was only about fifteen years old, that I wanted to be first in line. My biggest accomplishment is being able to buy that thing back."

Peter still has his family farm in Jayuya, where he grows several varieties of plantains. He hopes it will serve as a destination for fresh Puerto Rican food someday. Just one of many dreams for this *jibaro*.

Jibarito

Peter's recipe calls for a total of five total cloves of smashed garlic for one sandwich. Personally, I think cooking the beef in one clove of smashed garlic is adequate, so adjust per your personal taste. Jibaritos are a bit like French fries; they should be eaten immediately and turn soggy if cold.

Ingredients

1 green plantain

Corn oil

5 cloves smashed garlic

4–6 oz. thinly sliced sirloin

Adobo seasoning

Sliced onions (Spanish yellow preferred)

2 slices American cheese

2 slices tomato

Romaine lettuce

1 Tbsp. mayonnaise

Directions

1. Heat about 1 inch of oil to 300° in a frying pan.
2. While oil is heating, peel the plantain and cut it in half lengthwise.
3. Fry plantain halves at 300° F until they float. Float for 1–2 minutes. Monitor the temperature carefully; if it is too low, the plantains will be oily.
4. Drain plantains by setting on paper towels for 1–2 minutes.
5. Once the plantains are drained, transfer to cutting board and smash with a wooden block.*
6. In a separate sauté pan, heat 1–2 tablespoons of corn oil. Add 4 cloves smashed garlic. Cook until soft, about 2–3 minutes.
7. Sprinkle beef with adobo and place in pan with oil and garlic. Cook 2–3 minutes on each side or until preferred doneness. Add onion slices to pan, cook for another minute until lightly browned.
8. Put plantains back into oil, raise temperature to 325°. Fry for 3 minutes, longer if you prefer more crispy. Drain on paper towels.
9. To assemble sandwich, put one of the plantain slices down, layer two slices of cheese on top, add steak and onions, tomatoes, and lettuce. Spread mayo on the top piece of plantain, place on top.
10. Take a drop of corn oil, add 1 clove smashed garlic, mix, drizzle on top of sandwich. Dust top with adobo, cut in half, serve immediately.

Makes one sandwich.

*Must be smashed with something with a flat surface, not round like a rolling pin.

Six

RED APPLE BUFFET
A Pillar in Polonia

Imagine driving past a restaurant with a sign advertising "all-you-can-eat buffet." For many of us, this is likely to conjure up images of taste-less food made in mass quantities and left to languish under heat lamps for hours. Imagine seeing another sign for a restaurant serving "fresh, homemade food with seasonal, organic ingredients." The two restaurants seem as far apart as "foodie" and "buffet," right? However, these concepts aren't necessarily mutually exclusive; they've coexisted in harmony at Red Apple Buffet on Chicago's Northwest Side since 1989.

Czerwone Jabłuszko opened at 3121 North Milwaukee Avenue in Chicago's Avondale neighborhood in 1989. A second location at 6474 North Milwaukee in Norwood Park followed a year later. Owners Anna and Ferdynand Hebal started calling their restaurant by its English name, Red Apple Buffet, in the 1990s, since most people driving by didn't realize it was a restaurant—or a buffet, at that.

Some say that *bufets* were among the earliest Polish-owned businesses in Chicago (Granacki 2004, 81). Anna, who came to Chicago from Katowice, Poland, in 1982, is several generations younger than the city's first Polish immigrants and isn't familiar with these early *bufets*. "In the era that we grew up in, everything was owned by the government," she says of her homeland. "Restaurants were scarce. When we came to this country, we saw the buffets and thought, this is a great idea. It's like walking into paradise!" The all-you-can-eat buffet concept was more widespread in America throughout the 1970s and 1980s, remembered Anna. "It was popular and appealing. Now, they're hard to find. So, who's left? Only people who are crazy like us who have all-you-can-eat homemade food."

Small-Batch Buffet

Anna, a vivacious, energetic presence, is amazed that the Hebal's life-long approach to cooking—homemade food created with seasonal, organic, fresh ingredients—has finally caught on in Chicago. As a young girl growing up in 1960s Poland, Hebal says, "there were no GMOs, no nitrites, no antibiotics, additives, nothing. There was fresh. You could go to the market and purchase produce from the top organic growers. We grew up in an eco-friendly environment. There were no plastic bottles in Poland. There were no plastic bags."

Anna was also used to eating seasonal fruits and vegetables. "Winter, you don't have any tomatoes. How can you grow any tomatoes in winter in Poland? There were hothouses, but not too many. So, tomatoes were canned." Before winter arrived, says Anna, they would pickle everything. "Sauerkraut is pickled cabbage. In the old days, Poles ate pickled, dried foods and preserves. Dinner was meat and potatoes. We didn't have fresh salads."

Upon arriving in Chicago in the early '80s, Anna and Ferdynand were stunned to find the wide variety of produce available year-round. "When we came here, everything was in supermarkets, and it was amazing. Seen in the middle of hardcore winter, in January, the strawberries. But guess what, they didn't taste the same, because they were grown in hothouses, or shipped from other parts."

Ever since they started out, the Hebals have been sourcing their produce from Midwestern farmers. "We were always 'farm-to-table,'" insists Anna, both thrilled and a little amused that farm-to-table cuisine—a concept she has delivered to her customers since 1989—is now a culinary trend. "When we came here, we didn't know any other way. So when you're eating our blueberry pierogi, the blueberries are from Michigan, straight from the farm, picked by our hands." Offering fresh, homemade food is a challenging way to run any restaurant, much less one that's all-you-can-eat. "It's so hard!" admitted Anna. "Because you want to have frozen stuff reheated and put on the buffet so you have peace of mind, right? But this is not what we do here. That's probably how we survived."

Red Apple was recognized in 2016 as one of the top all-you-can-eat buffets in the country by both Time Out America and Tabelog.us, on the same list as buffet Goliaths such as Bacchanal and Wynn in Las Vegas, a city notorious for its over-the-top gourmet buffets. Despite the national attention, Anna knows that she still has a long way to go to overcome the stigma of the all-you-can-eat buffet. "There's like a mentality of oh, buffet, you put the food there, and it's staying there and it's getting old and it's all fried. And now there's just a new wave of interest in all-you-can-eat restaurants. We survived, because we're serving this every day, cooked fresh . . . every hour, freshly cooked food."

Rather than the large stainless steel bins typically found at buffets, Red Apple's food is presented in small, ceramic dishes that only hold about four to six portions at a time, the hot dishes heated by custom-built electric coils that run underneath. When cooks aren't watching over the buffet like hawks, turning over dishes several times a day, they're in the kitchen making small, fresh batches of food. In fact, the cooks are a common sight at the buffets, surveying what's needed or darting between customers to replenish empties, like pit stop mechanics at the Indy 500. Front-of-house staff are also on constant watch, sampling dishes and sharing feedback with the kitchen, making sure everything is up to standard. This is perhaps the largest distinction between Red Apple and a cliché buffet—small-batch cooking with fresh ingredients. It just happens to be served in an all-you-can-eat, buffet format. The best of both worlds, really.

Pan-European with a Polish Focus

Distinguishing Polish food from other types of European cuisine is difficult. Poland's borders and territories have been redrawn, carved up, and claimed by different European governments throughout its tumultuous history. Poland disappeared from Europe's map altogether from 1795 to 1918, when it was partitioned among Prussia, Russia, and Austria; it then fell under Soviet rule after World War II until it regained independence in 1989.

Anna calls her menu "pan-European, with a Polish focus." Customers with roots in Germany, Austria, Russia, France, Ukraine, Romania, Hungary, and Poland will all find tastes of home at Red Apple. Dishes can change throughout the week, even throughout the day, though Anna knows she must always keep a fresh supply of foods found in traditional Polish homes such as cheese blintzes, apple pancakes, and stuffed cabbage.

When she and Ferdynand first opened Red Apple, they called their friends and family back in Poland to acquire much-needed recipes. The pork stew and pierogi dough recipes are from Ferdynand's family. The apple cake and beef goulash are from Anna's side. The chiffon pumpkin pie was something Anna first tasted at a friend's house. She begged and pleaded for the recipe, then started to offer it to her family every Thanksgiving. Now it's at Red Apple, along with the same friend's heavenly cheesecakes. "We have tons of recipes we've incor-

Ferdynand and Anna Hebal, with daughter Magdalena

porated over the years from one or the other side of our families, or our close friends, and even one or two recipes from our employees," says Anna, whose staff are primarily from Eastern Europe.

When asked if any of her recipes have been adapted over the years for American tastes, Anna stopped to consider the idea, as though for the first time. "Maybe I should?" she asked. After another moment or two, she shook her head, banishing the thought. "No. Because it's . . . it's good. It's just good!" No argument there, I thought. And no need to alter recipes that have been cherished by several generations of Eastern European and American families.

What's Old Is New

Some of the ingredients central to Polish cooking are potatoes, mushrooms, and beets. Anna is ecstatic to witness the newfound popularity of beets—a root vegetable that was rarely found in Chicago restaurants until about 2005 or so. "There is a renaissance of beets. Finally! Hallelujah!" she exclaims. "Beets, they've never been popular. In our restaurant for years, there's plenty of beets. We have a cold beet soup for summer. We have a warm creamy beet puree, which is absolutely delicious. We have beets with horseradish. We have marinated beets with oregano and onion and vinegar and oil . . . absolutely delicious. Our spinach and beet salad . . . it's so popular now."

A stroll over to the buffet at either Red Apple location (both feature similar spreads) presents an array of choices that would overwhelm the heartiest of appetites. Among the hot dishes are daily fish specials, such as tilapia or pollock. Then there are the mouthwatering pierogi—one of the main reasons why many come to Polish restaurants (including this writer). On any given day, diners will find at least three varieties of handcrafted pierogi out at a time, from strawberry, blueberry, and sweet cheese, to potato and cheese, kishke (blood sausage and barley), or mushroom and sauerkraut.

There are also Eastern European classics, such as stuffed cabbage, sausage and onions, paprikash, schnitzel, sauerkraut—made with caraway, a traditional German style—meatballs in dill sauce, and mushroom gravy. The potato is omnipresent, offered mashed, boiled, and in dumplings and pancakes. There are even a few non-Polish favorites such as fried rice and pasta, to keep everyone at the table happy. On the weekends, when the price per head goes up by only a few bucks, there's succulent roast duck at the carving station.

Diners can also fill up on cold dishes such as coleslaw, herring, cucumber salad, red cabbage, pâté, and beets served several ways, along with beaucoup salad fixings. There's also fresh country bread—baked daily onsite—and real butter ("*never* margarine," insists Anna, whose svelte frame belies her livelihood). And lots and lots of horseradish. Latinos have jalapeños, Asians have wasabi, Anna says. Europeans who want to add heat to their food add a dab of horseradish, which can deliver a kick no other hot sauce or hot pepper can match.

Did I mention the desserts?

Eastern Europeans are known for their delectable, eye-pleasing cakes, cookies, and pastries. Dozens of different types of sweets are beautifully displayed at Red Apple Buffet, all, surprisingly, made onsite. From madeleines to flan to baked pear in homemade caramel and raisins (rum-soaked on the weekends), to the light, flaky apple strudel and delicate layered cakes decorated with nuts or fruits. Rum balls. Pudding. Everything is made from recipes lovingly handed down from friends and family back in Poland. The same ingredients, the same preparation methods—Anna teaches them all to her staff, who follow them to the letter. Neatly printed labels clearly identify each dish at the buffet. They don't always get updated when a dish is replaced—a problem willingly swapped for the constant turnover of fresh, homemade food.

Imported Beer, *Po Polsku*

When Red Apple first opened in 1989, imported and craft beers hadn't quite reached the mainstream in Chicago. Anna has witnessed the craft beer revolution unfold and notes that locals are now willing to shell out around ten dollars for a Belgian beer. "People are willing to pay, because they want to try it," she observed. "Some of them are good, some okay. But these beers," she says, pointing to the array of Polish beers on her menu, "a-ma-zing! We are trying to popularize them, because some of them are superb."

The craft beer craze in Poland started sometime around 2011. Aleksandera Zimoch, manager at European Imports, Red Apple's beer importer, started to see a few of these beers hit the Chicago market in 2015. It's tough to import them into the United States, she says, since their pasteurization methods mean a shorter shelf life—around six months. "Importing craft beers is kind of difficult, because you have to sell it quickly. That's why not many people are interested in importing them," she says.

Red Apple buys any Polish craft beers they can get their hands on. In 2017, they were carrying beers from Amber, one of the few craft breweries with distribution in Chicago, as well as Polish bocks, porters, and *Hefeweizen*. With so few of Poland's craft beers coming into Chicago, though, the top three Polish beers sold in the city—Żywiec, Tyskie, and Okocim, all pilsner-like beers—don't seem to be in danger of being toppled by Polish craft beers anytime soon.

Red Apple features a full bar at both locations, stocked with not only Polish beers but a large variety of Polish vodkas and liqueurs. The cocktail menu includes the red apple martini, a delicious concoction of apple vodka, apple juice, and grenadine, rimmed with brown sugar and cinnamon and garnished with a razor-thin slice of—what else?—red apple.

Polonia in Chicago

The history of Polish immigration to Chicago is at least as old as the city itself. The number of Polish Americans in Chicago jumped from 40,000 in 1890 to over 400,000 in 1930, making Chicago the nation's largest Polonia at the time (Kantowicz 1995, 174). Polish culture has touched every generation of Chicagoans and every area of Chicago, from earlier settlements in neighborhoods such as Noble Square, Bridgeport, and Back of the Yards to subsequent communities established along Milwaukee Avenue. Chicago and the Polish community. The Polish community and Chicago. The two are inextricably linked, like sausage and onions.

Kasia's, the famous pierogi brand distributed throughout the United States, was started in Chicago by Kazimiera Bober, a Polish immigrant who came to the city in the '70s. Both a park and a major street in Chicago were named in honor of Casimir Pulaski, a Pole who commanded four regiments of cavalry during the American Revolution. The road between the Shedd Aquarium and the Adler Planetarium on Chicago's museum campus was named Solidarity Drive to honor Poland's independence. Statues along the drive honor Nicolaus Copernicus, the Polish mathematician and astronomer, and Thaddeus Kosciuszko, the Polish war hero who fought in the American Revolution.

Those who lived in Chicagoland early in Pope John Paul II's twenty-seven-year reign had the opportunity to see him celebrate Mass in Grant Park or, as I did, catch a glimpse of the Pontiff's motorcade racing through the Northwest Side during the same visit in 1979. Blink, and you missed him as he sped by, waving to an adoring throng. Witnessing Chicagoland's peaceful, joyous Catholic Polish community en masse was one of the most amazing experiences I had growing up in Chicagoland. A once-in-a-lifetime event.

Polish Downtown

To see where Poles settled in Chicago, one needs only to look skyward to find one of the many church steeples, spires, and bell towers that have become a part of the city's landscape. A total of about sixty Catholic and Polish National Catholic churches were built in Chicago's Archdiocese in the nineteenth and twentieth centuries (Zurawski 2007, 4). Many of these churches continue to offer Mass in Polish, more than one hundred years after they were built.

St. Stanislaus Kostka was the first Polish parish in Chicago. Modeled after a church in Krakow, it opened at 1351 West Evergreen in the Noble Square neighborhood in 1867. Holy Trinity was founded a couple of blocks away in the 1870s; it was rebuilt in 1906 at 1118 North Noble, where Masses were still being said in Polish in 2017. Poles called this area "Stanislowowo-Trojcowo" in reference to these Catholic parishes, two of the largest in the world. St. John Cantius, St. Mary of the Angels, St. Hedwig's, and Holy Innocents all were built nearby shortly thereafter to accommodate the parishioners who flooded into the area from the mid-1800s until about 1920, when the United States began to curtail immigration.

This area also became known as "Trojska Polska," or Polish Downtown, and was centered at Ashland, Milwaukee, and Division. By 1890, nearly half of all Poles in Chicago had settled in Polish Downtown; it was the capital of America's Polonia from the late 1800s through the first half of the twentieth century. The storefronts on Noble and Milwaukee were filled with Polish-owned businesses. The headquarters for nearly every major Polish organization in America was located here, from the Polish National Alliance, to the Polish Roman Catholic Union of America and the Polish American Council, which was recognized as the central agency for Polish war relief. It is also the home of the world-famous Polish Museum of America. Among the museum's collections are artifacts from the Polish Pavilion at the 1939 World's Fair in New York, which could not be returned to Poland after World War II broke out (Granacki 2004, 7, 50).

In the late 1950s, however, urban renewal projects meant the demolition of several homes and businesses in Polish Downtown. The construction of the Kennedy Expressway, which opened in 1960, also cleared thousands of residences and forced many from the area, though Holy Trinity and St. Stanislaus Kostka were narrowly spared (you can see St. Stanislaus while driving on the Kennedy, at the Division exit). Many residents also chose to leave their tight tenements in Polish Downtown for the brick bungalows and two-flats that beckoned farther northwest along Milwaukee, as far away as Niles. Chicago's City Council officially named Polish Downtown "Polonia Triangle" in 1976 with a memorial in Noble Square, but by that time most Polish residents and organizations had moved to other parts of Chicagoland.

Milwaukee Avenue runs for more than forty miles, from downtown Chicago near Lake and Canal until it joins U.S. Route 41 and ends in Gurnee, Illinois. It was originally called Plank Road and served as a route for farmers delivering goods to the Randolph Street Market (Kaplan et al. 2014, 9). In the nineteenth and twentieth centuries, Poles settled primarily in neighborhoods along Milwaukee, from Polish Downtown to neighborhoods several miles north, such as Avondale, Portage Park, and Jefferson Park, and to northern suburbs such as Niles. Milwaukee Avenue is synonymous with Chicago's Polonia. Some even call this diagonal street the Polish Corridor. Case in point: Red Apple Buffet's two locations are more than four miles apart, yet they are both on Milwaukee.

Red Apple's location at 3121 North Milwaukee is in Avondale, which was a village before being annexed to the city of Chicago in 1889. Bounded roughly by Addison on the north, Diversey on the south, the Kennedy on the east, and Pulaski on the west, Avondale was a manufacturing hub for the first half of the twentieth century. Dad's Root Beer, Florsheim Shoes, Olson Rug, Maurice Lenell, and Henry Frerk & Sons all had factories there. Some of these factories were demolished for the construction of the Kennedy Expressway. Others, like Florsheim, were converted into residential condominiums. The building at the six-corner intersection of Diversey, Milwaukee, and Kimball, formerly the Hump Hair Pin Manufacturing Company and later the Morris B. Sachs department store, is now a historic landmark. It was renovated and renamed the Hairpin Lofts and Arts Center in 2011.

Approximately 100,000 Poles immigrated to Chicagoland between 1972 and 2000 (Erdmans 2006, 116). Throughout the 1970s and 1980s, Avondale was a gateway for this wave of Polish immigrants, many of whom left their homes after the collapse of the Soviet Union (Kaplan et al. 2014, 6). It was during this wave that Anna came to Chicago. "I left Poland, because everything was breaking down," she remembers. "Not slowly, but fast and surely. There were food stamps for everybody. The sugar was rationed. Everything was going really, really, really bad."

Anna (with red apple) and family in Katowice, Poland

Anna arrived in Chicago in 1982 with Magdalena, her daughter from her first marriage, only three-and-a-half years old at the time. She had visited Chicago once to see family friends and fell in love with the city. "I'm from Katowice, an industrial area, just like Chicago. So I kind of feel like I'm home in Chicago." Ferdynand also had left Poland with a son from his first marriage; the couple met in Chicago, married, and had another child, whom they named Ferdynand.

Poles were drawn to Avondale mainly because of St. Hyacinth's, a Catholic parish founded in 1894 near Milwaukee and Central. St. Hyacinth's was named a Basilica in 2004, partly to reflect the parish's history as the heart of the Catholic Polish community (Biemer 2004). It is now the largest Catholic Polish parish in Chicago. Many immigrants who came to Avondale from villages in Poland started calling the area around St. Hyacinth's "Jackowo," which roughly translates to Hyacinthville. They also started calling the area surrounding St. Wenceslaus parish, several blocks further north, "Wacławowo." Jackowo and Wacławowo are collectively known as Chicago's Polish Village. However, Jackowo is much more well-known to Poles outside of Chicago, who see it as a veritable home away from home.

Polish Americans represented the majority of the population in Avondale and other Northwest Side neighborhoods until about 2000, when these areas become predominantly Hispanic. On Jackowo's commercial strip, which runs on Milwaukee from Diversey to Addison, Modelo is now the best-selling beer at Polish-owned liquor stores. Signs proclaiming MOWIMY PO POLSKU (we speak Polish) and JACKOWO have largely disappeared, as Spanish has become more and more common. Jackowo is still a destination for the Polish-speaking community, however, as they can buy groceries, ship packages, seek medical care, and shop at one of the many businesses where Polish is still the primary language. In fact, businesses in this area typically greet me in Polish, as Avondale is the only neighborhood I've researched for this book in which I might be confused as a "local."

Other Centers of Polonia

A sizable Polish population also settled in Chicago's Jefferson Park neighborhood, centered at Lawrence and Milwaukee. The Copernicus Cultural Center on Lawrence, which features Polish cultural programs and performances in an 1,860-seat theater, took over the Gateway Theater in 1979. The exterior of the building was modified to resemble the Royal Castle in Warsaw; a white eagle, the national symbol of Poland, is perched atop the building's spire. The center has also hosted the Taste of Polonia, an annual festival of Polish food, culture, and entertainment, since 1979.

Central and Belmont is another area considered a center of Polonia in Chicago. The Portage-Cragin Chicago Public Library, on Belmont just west of Cicero, houses the second largest Polish-language collection in the city. In 2000, half of the population in this area was Polish, more than three-quarters of them immigrants. South of Belmont, the Polish population decreases while the Latino population increases. Businesses in this area tend to use the term "European" rather than "Polish" to attract an increasingly diverse population (Erdmans 2006, 122).

The Hebals opened their second Red Apple Buffet at 6474 North Milwaukee in Norwood Park in 1990, when it was clear they needed another location to serve the Polish Corridor farther north. Norwood Park has always been a residential community, initially settled by Germans, Poles, and Scandinavians. This far north, Milwaukee crisscrosses with other major streets such as Elston and Devon, near the famous Super Dawg drive-in. The Norwood Park Red Apple Buffet is slightly larger than its sister location, though both restaurants feature private dining rooms, a large collection of art commissioned from Polish artists, and bilingual staff to serve the Polish-speaking clientele.

A Gateway Restaurant

All throughout Chicago, however, Red Apple Buffet is known as one of the Polish community's crown jewels. Just as Avondale has been a gateway neighborhood for Polish immigrants, Red Apple Buffet is a gateway restaurant of sorts for those seeking their first taste of Polish culture in Chicago.

Dan Pogorzelski is the coauthor of several books, including *Avondale and Chicago's Polish Village*. He was also a tour guide with Chicago's Office of Tourism, concentrating on the history of Polish neighborhoods on Chicago's Northwest Side. "The Red Apple really helps . . . bring together Chicago's Polish community," he said from his office on none other than Milwaukee Avenue. "The same way that Chicago's Polish Village was a gateway for Poles from the 1960s on, for many people, that first meal would be the Red Apple. Some people feel very Polish, some people just want to embrace and taste Polish culture. The Red Apple is the place to do it."

Pogorzelski, who is also a former executive director of the Greater Avondale Chamber of Commerce, has taken out-of-town guests, media, and artists to Red Apple so they can experience its homemade food firsthand. "When artists come in to Chicago, we'll say, 'Where can we take them to eat?' Anna is always happy to help them. She's the informal mayor of Chicago's Polish Village."

Chicago's Polishness

Since about 2005, the number of Poles immigrating to the United States has slowed to a trickle. Several reasons are cited. There are better job opportunities in Poland, thanks to its 2004 entrance into the EU. Poles are also relocating to the United Kingdom, where higher-paying jobs are plentiful. Stricter immigration laws in place since September 11, 2001, have also kept many Poles from entering—or staying in—the United States.

Avondale is reinventing itself once again. "I'm witnessing a totally new era," Anna says. "We've been through the Solidarity era, lots of Polish businesses, then a new wave of immigrants from Mexico and Latin America and now, again . . . But we are very stubborn, we are still here. We think it's a great neighborhood, it's close to downtown, lots of potential," she says of Avondale. "Now they're renovating everything. Water lines. Infrastructure. Avondale's getting to be a hot region. It's just like Soho in New York, remember? The hipsters came first. And after hipsters, the wave of young families. And after families, another wave of investors, because people want to buy the properties here, and open up new restaurants, breweries, and all different businesses."

To Anna, Chicago's Polonia is like the wind: it has drifted down Milwaukee and out into the suburbs. Chicago's Polonia hasn't thinned out, said Pogorzelski, it's dispersed throughout Chicagoland. The majority of Polish Americans in Chicagoland now live in the suburbs, continuing a trend that began with the residents of Polish Downtown in the 1950s.* "You have more immigrants from Poland who settled in New York City" than the city of Chicago, he said, "but here in Chicago, that Polish presence is felt the way it isn't anywhere else in the United States. In terms of that feeling in Chicago . . . you feel that Polishness the way you don't in another place."

Pogorzelski finds this Polishness—a term Anna also uses frequently—at Red Apple. He likens a meal at Red Apple to one cooked in a traditional Polish home. "One of the most important things about Red Apple is that the food is extremely fresh. I think that definitely sets it apart from many other restaurants in general, that passion for freshness. When people are looking for their idea of Polish food, they'll find it there."

---

*There is a common belief that the city of Chicago still has the largest Polish population outside of Warsaw. While no one disputes that Chicago's Polonia is one of the strongest, if not the strongest, in the world, other cities may have eclipsed its population numbers at certain points in history (Dukes 2015).

Ferdynand Hebal Jr. makes pierogi

A Labor of Love

The Hebals' three children all chose different career paths from those of their parents. One is an architect, one is a computer scientist, the other a doctor. "We don't know to whom we should pass this business. We'll see, maybe granddaughters," Anna says, laughing. Her theory is that first-generation family members in America are like pioneers. The second generation, she surmises, wants its own identity, and the third longs for the traditions and customs of its ancestors, like the family restaurant. "Who knows?" she shrugs, adding later, "It's not easy. The restaurant business is very, very, very hard."

Pogorzelski has witnessed the same thing. "You don't find Polish restaurants in chichi Manhattan. These are labors of love. The reason why the White Eagle sold is because none of the kids wanted to do it anymore," he said, referring to White Eagle Banquets, a Polish-owned banquet hall in Niles (on Milwaukee Avenue, of course) opened in 1947 by Ted Przybylo. Ted's children took over after he passed away, but they decided to sell it to Victoria Banquets in 2015, marking the end of an era. "Once the founder goes," said Pogorzelski, "oftentimes that labor of love is not shared by their children."

In business since 1989, Red Apple has seen multiple generations of customers; people who came in when Red Apple first opened are now bringing their children. One of the cooks, Janina, has been with Red Apple since 1991, tending over the legacy of family recipes and serving as the proverbial "buffet hawk." Other employees have been with the Hebals for twenty years or more, starting as servers and now working in management. Ferdynand mostly handles the behind-the-scenes aspects of the business, while Anna zips back and forth between the two locations, serving as owner, operator, and ambassador. The areas surrounding both locations have shifted time and time again throughout the years, while not much has changed at Red Apple, other than the CZERWONE JABŁKO sign and the all-you-can-eat buffet's price, which was only $3.85 a head when they opened their doors. It was still quite affordable—well under twenty dollars—nearly thirty years later.

How does a small, family-owned business manage to land on the same "best buffets in America" lists as Bacchanal and Wynn? "Because we do everything ourselves," Anna says. "Old American way. Because we're first line of immigrants. We came here. We choose this country to be our country. We weren't born into it. This American dream, and this way of living, and this opportunity . . . everything is so precious to us. And should be to everyone who's coming to this country."

Even with all of the changes along the Polish Corridor, nothing, not even time, will ever remove the Polishness from Chicago. Poles have left their imprint all along Milwaukee Avenue, in its churches, its parks, its bakeries, and restaurants like Red Apple Buffet.

Paczki Day

In Poland, there is a tradition of making *paczki* (pronounced *poonch-key*), doughnut-like pastries filled with custard or fruit, on the Thursday before Lent, to clear houses of sugar, lard, and fruit—all forbidden during Lent.

Polish-owned bakeries in Chicago adopted this tradition, selling *paczki* on Mardi Gras, or Fat Tuesday, instead. Places like Oak Mill Bakery, which has locations in Niles and other areas around Chicagoland. Oak Mill sells tens of thousands of these delicious treats on what has become known as "Paczki Day" in Chicago. The bakery offers traditional fruit- and custard-filled varieties, but it has branched out with about two dozen different fillings, from Nutella to poppyseed to caramel and sea salt.

Glorious Fall Plum Tart

Eastern European chefs are well-known for their delicate, eye-pleasing desserts. This delicious recipe was handed down from Anna's mother, Olga.

Ingredients

Filling

6 oz. baker's cheese*
4 Tbsp. sunflower oil
2 Tbsp. honey
1 egg (you can substitute 2–2½ oz. milk)
12 oz. light wheat flour
1 Tbsp. baking powder (11 g)
3 lb. plums

Topping

4 oz. cold butter
4 oz. ground hazelnuts
3 Tbsp. honey
1 tsp. cinnamon
Extra butter for baking sheet

Directions

1. Preheat oven to 400° F.
2. Mix the baker's cheese with oil, honey, and egg, preferably by hand (if using an electric mixer, use a very slow speed). Combine the flour with baking powder and add this slowly to your cheese mixture to form the dough. Wrap the dough in plastic wrap and put it into the refrigerator for about 1 hour.

3. After 1 hour, spread the dough thinly onto a buttered cookie sheet. Cut the plums in half, discard the pits, and neatly arrange the halves on top of the dough.

4. Prepare the topping: Combine the hazelnuts, honey, and cinnamon, and with a knife cut the cold butter into this mixture. (To achieve proper consistency, do not handle the butter.) Crumble over plums.

5. Bake for 30–45 minutes, or until plums are soft.

6. Let cool for 5–10 minutes before serving.

*Baker's cheese is similar to cottage cheese or ricotta. It can be found in specialty grocery stores.

Seven

HEMA'S KITCHEN
Doyenne of Devon

Hema Potla had a very full life in Hyderabad, India. Both of her parents were educators. She had nine brothers and sisters. She was married to a successful man, held a university degree, and ran a lucrative business. But something called Hema to Chicago in 1981 to pursue the dream of owning her own business in America. None of her siblings or parents migrated to the United States; her husband didn't join her for more than a year. Why did Hema leave almost everything she had and journey to Chicago? "I was in a strange land. But I was never afraid."

Mother of the Year

When I sit down with Hema Potla, the owner and head chef of Hema's Kitchen, a fixture in Chicago's Little India neighborhood since 1991, I usually pepper her with a lot of questions. Why did you leave India? Why did you come to Chicago? What spices are in this dish? What spices are not in this dish?

But it's hard to ask someone questions when plate after plate of freshly made, delicious Indian food keeps arriving at your table. Hema, I'll say, I can't possibly eat all this food. I always urge her to let me know if she needs to attend to her restaurant, as we typically talk for hours. "Jean," she'll respond, each word dripping with her beautiful Indian accent, "the only problem is that you haven't eaten your food," even though I've been diving into aromatic, fork-tender chicken tikka masala and tearing off pieces of fresh, tandoor-baked naan between my questions. My polite protests are ignored. The plates keep coming.

Hema's Kitchen has drawn a loyal following for decades. Though she is from southern India, both of Hema's restaurants (a second location, Hema's Kitchen II, opened at 2411 North Clark in 2003) primarily serve northern Indian cuisine. Hema is a darling of the local press. *Chicago* magazine once named Hema's Kitchen one of its top twenty restaurants in Chicago. *Chicago Reader* named it best Indian restaurant in 2014, and WGN-TV's "Chicago's Best" claimed Hema's as "best spicy" in 2015, to list a mere few.

Hema was a regular chef at Taste of Chicago for several years, and she held traditional Indian cooking demonstrations at the old Marshall Field's department store on State Street. She is celebrated for her culinary expertise by food critics like the late Pat Bruno, who declared in a *Chicago Sun-Times* article that Hema's Kitchen offers "the understanding of what makes great-tasting Indian food—spices. Owner/chef Hema Potla knows her Indian spices and uses them with abandon" (Bruno 2008).

What most people do not know about Hema Potla is that she devotes much of her time to religious and philanthropic activities. In 2002, she was given the Woman of the Year Award by Chicago-based International Congress of India Christians for building a church in Andhra Pradesh, her home state. Hema has been recognized by U.S. congressman Danny Davis for her humanitarian efforts in the community, earning a Mother of the Year award in 2014. She also has been honored for distinguished service by the National Federation of Indian American Associations, a nonprofit organization that has served the Indian American community since 1980. Considering that Hema keeps workaholic-level hours running two restaurants, these accomplishments are especially remarkable.

But Hema Potla is not interested in talking about her achievements or awards with me. The petite, raven-haired restaurateur, whose eyes sparkle and dance along with her bejeweled fingers, is far more interested in whether I am enjoying her food. While I eat, her eyes seem to follow my fork to my mouth, patiently waiting for my critique of each bite, which is usually profound and goes something like "Mmmmm." Hema knows that her potato samosas, delicately fried pastry shells stuffed with tender veggies and fragrant spices, are my favorite, and she never lets me leave without at least one serving to go. As I leave, there are hugs, best wishes, and bags of leftovers proffered. It's not hard to see why she's been called Mother of the Year.

From Tomboy to Entrepreneur

Hema Potla was born in the state of Andhra Pradesh, in southeastern India. Andhra Pradesh is named after the Andhra people, who developed their own language, Telugu, Hema's native tongue. The area is filled with forests, rivers, hills, and caves. One of Andhra Pradesh's major landmarks is the Venkateswara Temple in Tirumala, an ornate hilltop shrine to the god Vishnu. It attracts millions of worshippers annually.

Growing up in Hyderabad, the capital of Andhra Pradesh, Hema had no interest in cooking. Her famous line is, "I didn't even know how to boil water." The sixth of ten children, Hema describes her younger self as a tomboy who was happier running around outside instead of making lentils in the kitchen. If her parents, who were both grade-school principals, needed something, Hema would be the first to run out and get it. Then, around the age of fifteen, she started to cook with whatever ingredients were in the kitchen. "I used to make my own dishes," she says. "Experiment. Most of the time it would turn out very good, and people liked it. It became a passion."

Decades later, Hema no doubt found her calling as a chef and restaurateur. But it was a long, winding path to get there.

Hema met her husband, Sam Potla, in her teens. They were married two years after they met. When I asked Hema if it was an arranged marriage, she blushed and said, "Sort of, because he liked me before."

Hema's smile is omnipresent. But when she speaks of her late husband Sam, her smile recedes into her face as though remembering a well-kept, cherished secret. Two years after meeting Sam, Hema saw him again. "I was a high-school graduate by that time. In India, you cannot get married before you are eighteen."

A few years after they married, Hema earned a degree in economics from Osmania University in Hyderabad. "The degree is something I wanted to have, like any of my friends," she says. "It was a personal goal. It gives you more opportunity to go into things." As long as she can remember, Hema saw herself as an entrepreneur. "I always wanted a business for myself. So, in that way, my degree helped." The Potlas moved from Hyderabad to Bombay, now Mumbai, where Sam served in the Indian navy. Hema ran a business from home selling saris and cosmetics to their military friends.

After ten years, the couple moved back to Hyderabad, where Hema decided to build on the cottage industry she started on the naval base. She opened Hema's Beauty Shoppe, which was a successful business for thirteen years, employing seventeen people at its peak. "It was all things under one roof," Hema explains. "Textiles, cosmetics, tailoring, clothing, and beauty shop." Shortly after, their daughter, Prameela ("Pam"), was born—the city's first baby on New Year's Day, 1969. "If my mother is upset, she will call me 'Prameela!'" Pam says, laughing, mirroring her mother's charisma and generous nature. "Otherwise, I am good with 'Pam.'"

After the United States eased Asian immigration restrictions in 1965, Indians started traveling to America, including many of Beauty Shoppe's customers. Indian families are moving to cities like Chicago, they reported back to Hema. They're making a living providing specialized services to the growing Indian communities there—services such as tailoring and cosmetics, the types of services Hema excelled at. "They used to tell me, 'What are you doing here? Come to America. You are so talented. You must come to America.'"

Hema's customers gave her the telephone numbers of friends and relatives in Chicago. They persisted, insisting that she bring her business to American soil. The dream of running a business in America bit Hema hard. She started pestering her husband. "I said, 'I want to go, I want to go. I want to see. I want to start a business there.' He said

'No, it'll be too hard for you to start a business there.' I was thinking, what is so hard, when I can do business here?" Hema was determined to duplicate her shop's success in Chicago.

"He Thought I'd Be Back within Four Months"

Armed with fistfuls of Chicago contacts from Beauty Shoppe customers, Hema moved to Chicago with twelve-year-old Pam in 1981. Obtaining a work visa, she says, was rather easy. Sam stayed in India. "He stayed, because he was working abroad, but he said, 'OK, I'll take care of the business here. You go.' He thought, let her go and have a look. He thought I'd be back within four months."

Good fortune would have to wait. As soon as Hema arrived, she experienced her first lesson in distrust. "I brought four boxes of things with me to start a store," she remembers. "People bought everything, but they never paid." A month, two months, then six months passed, without anyone paying Hema for the goods she sold. "I crossed all the oceans, and I came here, thinking people are going to help me. All the people who gave me their telephone numbers, they didn't even bother to pick up the phone." Hema finally reconciled with her loss and took a stab at entering the motel business, but things never materialized.

After fifteen months passed, Sam, then retired from the navy and doing charitable work in Hyderabad, realized that his wife wasn't returning to India. He turned Hema's Beauty Shoppe over to her youngest sister and joined Hema and Pam in West Rogers Park.

"I have only one daughter," Hema says about her permanent move from India to Chicago. "Then Sam came, after fifteen months. He came in '82. There was still property there, plenty of property there in India. But when I, my husband, my daughter, we three were here, it's like my whole family is here. *My* family. My brothers, sisters, that is a different thing. I didn't go back."

After realizing that a Chicago version of Hema's Beauty Shoppe wasn't in the cards, Hema knew she would have to work for someone else to make a living. Though she lacked any formal culinary training or on-the-job experience, Hema was able to get a job in the kitchen at an Indian restaurant on Devon. "I'm a good worker, I can learn fast. Then they realized I can become a good chef." She worked as a chef's assistant for a year before moving on to Klay Oven at 414 North Orleans in Chicago's River North neighborhood, where she worked on the line from 1988 to 1990 (the location on Orleans has since closed, though a new location, Klay Oven Kitchen, opened in 2012 at the French Market on Clinton Street). The dream of owning her own business—this time, a restaurant—reappeared on the horizon.

When Sam arrived in the United States, Hema helped him open a candy store next to the Kedzie CTA train station. In the mornings, Hema would work at the candy store with her husband, then take the El to Klay Oven, where she worked a full shift. Sam became well known throughout the West Rogers Park neighborhood as a kind, gentle soul. But he lacked Hema's business sense, and the candy store was soon shuttered. "I opened it [the candy store] for him, because I was working for Klay Oven. We lost money on that . . . like, $34,000. That's a lot of money for me."

Though she was juggling motherhood, a failed family business, and a stressful restaurant job, Hema doesn't complain about those years. "God is good to me," she says, a phrase oft-spoken when recalling trying times in her life. But after four years working for others, Hema was ready to open her own restaurant.

West Rogers Park Comes into Its Own

Hema's Kitchen was originally a forty-seat eatery at 6406 North Oakley, just a few blocks east from its current spot at 2439 West Devon. Both locations are in Chicago's West Rogers Park neighborhood, which is also referred to as West Ridge or North Town. Hema only knows her neighborhood as Rogers Park and seems perplexed at the suggestion of any other name. (For consistency's sake, I will refer to this area as West Rogers Park.) It is bordered on the north by Howard; the east by Ridge Boulevard, Ravenswood Avenue, and Western; the south by Peterson and Bryn Mawr; and the west by the North Shore Channel and Kedzie (Day and Santoro 2008, 10).

After 1893, when West Rogers Park and Rogers Park—collectively known as Chicago's Far North Side—became a part of the city of Chicago, immigrants seeking affordable housing flocked to West Rogers Park. The newly annexed Far North Side prompted the city to establish a new street numbering method in 1908. The system, which is still in use, established State and Madison as ground zero points, with even-numbered addresses on the north and west sides of the streets and odd-numbered addresses on the south and east sides. The method also established the basic unit of 800 to signify one mile (Samors et al. 2001, 42).

As immigrants continued to pour into West Rogers Park, its population grew from only 300 in 1891 to 7,500 in 1920. Realtors coined the name "West Rogers Park" in the 1920s to capitalize on the Rogers Park name, which signified wealth and prestige (Day and Santoro 2008, 24, 57). A strong Jewish population started to take hold in West Rogers Park around this time, as it was more welcoming to Jews than other parts of the city. The Devon Avenue cable-car line, which ran from Western to Kedzie (also referred to by locals as the streetcar) started running in 1925, bringing more development to the area, which had lagged behind its Rogers Park neighbor because of a lack of public transportation (Samors et al. 2001, 64).

West Rogers Park experienced a housing boom from 1920 until about 1930. During this time, the population grew from 7,500 to more than 40,000, leveling out with the onset of the Depression (Day and Santoro 2008, 57). Throughout the 1940s, the western part of West Rogers Park remained mostly undeveloped. This included Devon west of California and the section bordered by Western, Touhy, Kedzie and Howard, which was mostly prairie. West Rogers Park's two established commercial areas were Western and Devon avenues; both featured several movie theaters and restaurants (Samors et al. 2001, 122).

The post–World War II era brought another housing boom and a burst of development to West Rogers Park. Cook County Federal Savings opened at 2326 West Devon in 1948 (Day and Santoro 2008, 98). When it was rebuilt in 1953 at Devon and Fairfield, the colonial-style structure became a hallmark of Devon, which was soon developed from Western to Mozart with stores, restaurants, and groceries. During the '40s, '50s, and '60s, Devon was considered one of the nicest streets in the city. People could shop, see a movie, go dancing, visit restaurants, or simply stroll down the street (Samors et al. 2001, 133).

In 1957, West Rogers Park led all other Chicago neighborhoods in new home construction rates, with 802 new living units. Rogers Park was a distant second, with 233. The residential housing boom subsided in the 1960s in West Rogers Park, but new store and business construction surged. Commercial buildings started to fill vacant lots on Devon between Western and California (Samors et al. 2001, 126).

Although West Rogers Park still boasted the largest Jewish population in Chicago in 1970 (Samors et al. 2001, 126), things started to shift on the Far North Side. Many Jewish families, particularly Reform Jews, left the area for the suburbs, with Assyrians, Greeks, Indians, Pakistanis, and Bangladeshis following in their wake. The area's Jewish population continued to diminish throughout the 1970s and into the 1980s. The area showed its age as buildings started to appear rundown, and the commercial district on Devon Avenue began to lose its luster (Day and Santoro 2008, 115).

Devon Transforms into Little India

From 1920 to 1960, nearly all immigrants to the United States were from Europe, Central America, or South America. Only 3 percent came from Asia. Immigration restrictions started to ease in the 1940s and 1950s, but it wasn't until 1965 that Congress enacted major reform, at the urging of both President Johnson and President Kennedy.

The U.S. Immigration and Nationality Act of 1965 loosened immigration restrictions and encouraged foreign-born U.S. citizens to sponsor family members. This propelled Asian Indians to immigrate to major urban areas such as Chicago. The act also provided visas to professionals such as doctors, scientists, and engineers, whose skills were in demand in the United States thanks to the Cold War and Vietnam War. Significant numbers of qualified Indians were recruited to cities such as Chicago to help remedy these talent shortages (Indo-American Center 2003, 9). This was a boon for English-speaking, highly educated Indians who faced a lack of opportunities back home (Rangaswamy 1995, 441).

As Jewish businesses in West Rogers Park moved to the suburbs or elsewhere in the city in the 1970s, Asian Indians streamed into the area, attracted to the area's "suburb in a city" environment, affordable housing, good parks and schools, and business opportunities (Day and Santoro 2008, 109, 113). Unlike other immigrant populations, Asian

Indians did not flee their homeland to escape religious persecution or extreme hardship (Indo-American Center 2003, 9). Asian Indians were fluent in English and educated in schools modeled on the British education system. They were comfortable with the business culture and work ethic found in the United States. The prospect of earning a higher education in the West also held great prestige (Rangaswamy 1995, 441).

West Rogers Park became a port of entry for Asian Indians, and Indian-owned businesses began to appear on Devon. India Sari Palace, the area's first sari store, opened on Devon in May 1973. Patel Brothers' first grocery store opened at 2034 West Devon in 1974 (it has since moved to 2610 West Devon). Patel Brothers is now a nationwide retail grocery chain.

By the mid-1980s, relatives sponsored under the family reunification clause of the 1965 immigration act began to arrive in Chicago. Many settled in West Rogers Park. Devon became an enclave for Indian food, culture, and products as Indian businesses flooded onto the 1.2-mile stretch of Devon from Ridge to California. Pakistani and Bangladeshi immigrants followed.

"Little India" on Devon Avenue

In 1980, the first year that Asian Indians were counted in the U.S. Census, the population of Asian Indians in Chicagoland was 31,858. It grew to 57,992 by 1990, 113,700 by 2000, and 186,000 by 2010, making Asian Indians the largest Asian group in Chicagoland (U.S. Census Bureau 2012).

Despite the dramatic changes in West Rogers Park's population, the area was still predominantly Jewish when Hema arrived in 1981. "When we used to walk on Devon, if we heard our own language (Telugu), we used to turn and look at them, because it was rare," she recalled. "Then, slowly, Indians started buying the stores." By the time she opened Hema's Kitchen in 1991, the Jewish population had started leaving, and Indian businesses were investing in the area, making improvements to the commercial district on Devon.

Historically, West Rogers Park has been a port of entry for many ethnic groups, making it one of the most diverse neighborhoods in Chicago. In addition to its strong Jewish, Indian, Pakistani, and Bangladeshi populations, the area has also attracted Eastern European, Middle Eastern, Caribbean, and Mexican populations. "It's like the United Nations over here," says Fozi Suleiman, the owner of Farm City Meat at 2255 West Devon since 1985. (Farm City is also Hema's primary meat vendor.)

Suleiman identified three distinct sections of Devon: From Kedzie to California, it's Jewish; from California to Western, it's Indian; from Western to Damen, it's Pakistani. Honorary Chicago street signs bolster Suleiman's assertions about Devon's diversity. On July 20, 1991, the section of Devon from California to Western was named Gandhi Marg (Way), dedicated to Mahatma Gandhi. The section from Kedzie to California is dedicated to former Israeli premier Golda Meir. A section from Western to Damen is Mohammed Ali Jinnah Way, dedicated to the founder of Pakistan, and yet another section, from Ravenswood to Damen, is Sheikh Mujib Way, in honor of Bangladesh's founder and first head of state.

Now, Hema says, hearing Telugu is no longer rare. "You find my own countrymen on Devon, you can find them everywhere. Now it is like an Indian street, a Little India." The Jewish population didn't disappear, she explains. Many moved further west, toward Sacramento. A multitude of synagogues remain in the area.

Hema's Kitchen: The Birth and Rebirth

On October 18, 1991, just a few months after a section of Devon was dedicated to Gandhi, Hema's Kitchen opened at 6406 North Oakley. Hema created the menu, did all of the made-to-order cooking in the small kitchen ("eating at Hema's was not a fast-food experience," joked one long-time customer), served the food, and even bused tables. "I had a big window, and they could come and watch," Hema says about her kitchen, which was visible to the dining room. "I took their order, went inside, cooked it for them . . . In those days, I was doing everything," she says, her face beaming with fond remembrance. "Dishwashing and cleaning up . . . And I did it very willingly . . . with happiness. It's my own. I love people, and they are good to me."

"When she started her business," says her daughter, Pam, "the neighborhood and the store owners, they said, 'She's going to close in six months.'" Pam's parents bought the business for $10,000. Her father was unsure how or when they were going to be able to pay back the loan. "My dad said, 'I'll pay you in two months,' because they didn't know how it was going to work out. In that month, the first month, they made $10,000. With Mom," continued Pam, who is in awe of her mother's strength and resilience, "she just has that in her. It is God's blessings. There's nothing else to it. People respect her so much. They don't call her Hema, they call her 'Hema-ji.' Ji is 'with respect.'"

Going to the original Hema's Kitchen was a bit like going to someone's home for dinner. Hema greeted her customers, cooked for them, and answered questions about the menu. There was even a playpen in a corner of the dining room, when grandsons Rahul and Rohan came to visit. "Yes, Pam would have them play in the playpen when they became toddlers. Customers would play with them when they were here," Hema says.

Sam became Hema's right-hand man at the restaurant. "He used to help me . . . in everything, from A to Z. As long as he was here, I didn't have to do the shopping for the restaurant. He used to do that for me. He was always there to give me advice. You know, if I wanted to start something, I would discuss it with him. He used to say, 'you can do it.' He always supported me."

She paused for a moment, then looked at me. "Jean, you need to eat your lunch."

There is the saying that tragedies happen in threes. I am reluctant to describe someone's hardships with a cliché. Yet that is the only way to preface the next phase of Hema's life. Three tragedies happened in the short period from 1994 to 1997.

In 1994, Sam was diagnosed with cancer. Hema's Kitchen was taking off, so Hema shuttled back and forth between the restaurant and their apartment, which was just across the street. "I would go home, take care of Sam, go back to the restaurant, go with him to the hospital for chemo treatments, go back to the restaurant . . . Pam was just out of high school. She was working at Walgreens and helping at the restaurant."

"It was horrible at that time," recalled Pam, her usually bubbly voice solemn. "I was working another job . . . I had insurance . . . I couldn't just leave it. I went to school . . . I would come and work in the restaurant and help her out. I'm the only child, no brothers, no sisters . . . Anytime there was anything going on in the family, we were all there for one another."

Then, the fire happened.

"I was working in the restaurant," remembers Hema. "A neighbor came running and said 'Hema, your house is on fire!' I ran across the street. We were living on the second floor of a six-unit building. The fire was throughout the entire building. They don't let you go in . . . Someone on the top floor died from smoke inhalation. Sam was out, he wasn't at home or at the restaurant. Half of my belongings were ruined. Smoke ruined things. I don't remember the cause. Salvation Army put us into a hotel for three days. We had a lot of trouble finding temporary housing. They would say, 'You can move back into your apartment in three months.' Then they would say, 'Maybe three more months.' We finally moved somewhere else."

Hema grabbed onto her faith and held tight during those years. She would need every ounce of the same strength and determination that led her to America, that helped her regroup after every failed business, that enabled her to open her own restaurant in a country that finally opened its doors to Asian immigrants.

In 1995, just four years after helping Hema realize her dream of owning her own business in America, Sam passed away at the age of sixty-one. "Twenty years since his death, people still remember him," Hema says, looking down at the table, her words carrying the gravity of remembering the love of her life. After a moment, she looks up. Her face brightens, her voice almost musical. "He's the best person, best father, best husband, best friend, best everything." She looks at me, nodding in agreement with each fond memory. "We had a very beautiful relationship."

Then, in 1997, while in Richmond, Virginia, Hema went for a walk.

She and Pam were in town for a conference and had just arrived at the convention center. "We got off our bus . . . We're all just talking, and I guess she wanted to cross the street," remembers Pam. "I just turned around and I heard a noise, and I see my mom *flying up*! She fell on the truck, and then she rolled . . ." Twenty years later, Pam still reels from the shock of the moment. "This happened in '97. I lost my dad to cancer in '95. I'm like, 'God, I can't lose my mom!'"

Hema suffered serious injuries, including a broken tibia. "I had surgery to reinforce my leg with a metal plate and screws. It took a year to heal," she says. Hema's Kitchen, now a one-woman show, had to shut down while Hema gained the strength to work again. "I had to close down, but I still had to pay the lease," she says, showing a rare display of bitterness. "I was paying, and I was waiting for my leg to get well. I am a tough woman, Jean. I am a survivor. I was in three disasters. But the good God gave me the strength to recover from all these things."

"She survived all of it," says Suleiman, who describes Hema as a "wonderful lady . . . a beautiful person. She had some health issues . . . that forced her to close her restaurant, but she survived."

"God has given us so much courage and stamina and willpower," added Pam, emphasizing that her mother is not someone who will get defeated from hardship. "She has that strength."

What happened next is nothing short of pure redemption. In its first six years of business, Hema's Kitchen managed to build a cult following. People all over the city and suburbs had developed a craving for flavorful Indian food served by a cheerful, motherly Indian woman who cooked with her heart and soul. On the day Hema's Kitchen reopened in 1998, exactly 364 days after the truck accident forced her to close, there was a line of customers waiting on the sidewalk.

"They came back when I opened the restaurant again," Hema recalled, her eyes still able to register the joyful surprise of seeing customers waiting for a seat at "Amma's" table. "They didn't let me down. They didn't forget about me. I give credit to my God, not myself only. All I had to do is give them fresh and good food. The rest, my God has done for me. Like my mom used to say, 'You do your best, God is going to do the rest.'"

Hearing of the reopening of the small storefront on Oakley, the media pounced on what was once a well-kept secret in Little India. A feature in *Chicago* magazine, Hema says, "doubled the business." Then *Check, Please!* came. "That doubled the business again. After that, every newspaper, Channel 7, Channel 2, Channel 5, 9, they all took care of me. It's a wonderful journey, all these years of my restaurant life. I can only say, God is good to me, and people didn't let me down." Even as Hema and I were talking at her restaurant on a winter day in 2016, a customer came in after seeing the *Check, Please!* segment, which had originally aired in 2001. About 95 percent of her customers are Caucasian, not Indian, says Hema. She credits this to the local media frenzy that started in 1991 with a segment on WGN-TV and escalated in the late 1990s.

Hema's Kitchen II, which seats about fifty, opened in Chicago's Lincoln Park neighborhood in 2003 to accommodate her growing clientele. Hema's Kitchen in West Rogers Park then moved down the street in 2007 to 2439 West Devon, a space that is about double the size of her original digs and features two tandoor ovens. No longer a one-woman show, Hema has several people working for her in the kitchen and dining room. "I am chef for both my restaurants," she says from a back table at the Devon restaurant, where she pays bills and returns phone calls. "If I start anything new, I teach my workers . . . and it works."

What's in That Vindaloo That You Do?

Hema's Kitchen's menu contains a staggering 105 menu items, enough to keep a regular sampling different dishes for years. "When we started in 1991, the menu wasn't this big," Hema says. "We keep changing it. Every year or two years, I take a look at it." Hema's mother influenced the southern Indian recipes she uses today, such as the dal with *baigan* (lentils cooked with eggplant).

Southern Indian cooks use more spices, she says, more chili powder. Vindaloo, a southern Indian dish, is the holy grail for diners seeking the hottest food they can find—the kind of heat that leaves you sweating, clearing your sinuses, gasping for relief. Vindaloo is a stewlike dish, made with a rich gravy of coconut milk, tomatoes, and vegetables. Its tremendously high level of heat, Hema explains, comes from red chili powder. "For regular dishes, I only use quarter teaspoon chili powder," she explained. "For vindaloo," she continued, with a mischievous smile on her face, "I use a whole spoon and a half. When they ask for the chicken vindaloo, lamb vindaloo, or fish vindaloo, we use a whole spoon and a half. If we use a little bit less, then they say, 'Hema, you cheated!'" she says, giggling, like the victor of a good prank. "I will modify our dishes if the customer wants medium or mild, but not vindaloo. A lot of Americans want the heat. It's like a challenge. They need to drink water, they go to the bathroom, they come back, they can't finish it."

If there is any misconception that Hema's American clientele prefers bland food, the vindaloo should clear that up.

Many other dishes on her menu, Hema says, are influenced by northern Indian cooking. "My husband was in the navy. I lived in Bombay [now Mumbai] for ten years, and I lived with the armed forces. Army, navy, and air force people. I lived with different sort of people in Bombay." It was there that Hema was first introduced to the flavors and recipes of northern Indian food.

About 50 percent of the menu, Hema says, consists of her own creations—dishes not found anywhere else, such as *aloo jeera*, *matar* mushroom, *sag chana*, *achari paneer aloo*, *buna gosht*, lamb with *baigan* and curry leaves, and *sag murg*. Others are commonly known but feature her own combination of spices, such as the kabobs rolled in paratha or *pulka* (hand-rolled homemade wheat breads) and *masala vada*. She also rotates her chef's specials with about a dozen "Hema's Sizzlers."

One of her creations, *haryali* chicken, joins the list of ethnically influenced dishes that were created in Chicago. *Haryali* ("green" in

Hindi) chicken is cooked in a spicy coconut sauce. "It's very popular," Hema beams. "You won't find it in other restaurants." Two other original creations are *dal palak* and *dal dahkni*, vegetarian entrees made with roasted yellow lentils. Lentils are a staple in Indian cooking, Pam explains. "They are in every day, on every table, in every house. Like rice." Besides many versions of dal, lentils are also used in Hema's mulligatawny soup, a delicious concoction made with herbs and her special blend of Indian spices.

Hema still experiments with recipes at her restaurant, much as she did in her mom's kitchen in Andhra Pradesh. She tests these recipes with staff, friends, and family at least "five or six times" before adding them to the menu. A peek into the large kitchen on Devon reveals several baker's racks filled with spices—spices that are roasted and ground onsite, a time-consuming process but necessary, Hema says, to achieve the complex flavors she is known for. The Devon location's two tandoor ovens are a luxury she did not have on Oakley Street. This has allowed her to expand the menu with tandoor-baked breads such as traditional naan, which takes less than two minutes in the 400–500 degree charcoal oven.

One of Hema's Kitchen's tandoor ovens

As Hema and I talked one day at her usual table at the Devon location, her employees—who hail from India and Mexico—checked in with her about myriad issues. She spoke in alternating Hindi, Urdu, Telugu, and Spanish. Her chef has been with her since 2003. Another employee started as a dishwasher when he was only fourteen. Thirteen years later, he is now part of the kitchen staff.

Even with all the distractions, Hema still fussed over me. "Is it too spicy for you?" she asked me, referring to the plate of chicken tikka masala at my side. "No!" I insisted. "It's good for my sinuses."

BYOB by Choice

I stumbled across some interesting statistics while writing *BYOB Chicago*, a guide to the bring-your-own-bottle dining scene in Chicagoland. I found, for example, that a little over half of all BYOB restaurants in Chicago *choose* to operate without a liquor license. That was surprising, particularly in an industry where alcohol sales equal profits. Hema Potla is one of those restaurateurs who chooses to have a BYOB policy. "I don't want a liquor license here," she says resolutely. Even in 1991, when she first opened, Hema knew that Chicagoans loved BYOBs. "When you make it BYOB," she offered, "it's automatically more popular. It was also because I was alone and wouldn't be able to control the bar. You have to trust a lot of people when you have a bar. I don't drink. Not even beer, wine, anything."

Hema's reasons for not drinking are cultural, not religious. "Indian ladies, we don't drink. When I was in India, it was the norm. Men drink and fall on the roads [*laughs*]. They get drunk. And not all the men. My husband used to do it very moderately. When he took a sip, when he smoked, you barely noticed. It's like a style. Very moderate. Not a drunk," she says solemnly about Sam. "Not a drunk."

A lot of BYOBs have problems. Customers continue to drink long after their meals are finished, taking business away from diners waiting for a table. Or they bring a large amount of alcohol, overindulge, and get sloppy drunk. Her customers have never given her a problem. "Not in Hema's Kitchen," she says. "They bring their own, they don't drink too much, they don't make a scene. If there is a big party of twenty-five people, they bring coolers, but they don't give us any problems. They're always good. We supply the glasses, we supply the opener, we supply the ice buckets, we give them everything, but we never charge for that."

Although Hema's BYOB policy is not primarily motivated by religion, other Indian- and Pakistani-owned BYOBs on Devon do credit religion for their decision to forgo a liquor license. This perhaps explains the limited number of liquor stores on Devon. If her customers are caught empty-handed, says Hema, she sends them down the street, where only one or two beverage retailers exist. This is hardly the case at the Lincoln Park locale, where liquor stores abound. "They behave, Jean," Hema says of her BYOB customers. "They know their own limit."

As we talked, Hema surveyed the steaming cup of tea in front of me.

"How is your chai?"

Hema-ji

Hema Potla has many names here in Chicago: Hema, Mom, Mommy, Hema-ji, and Amma. "Amma means Mom," explained Pam. "Some of the store owners . . . they'll call her Hema-ji. Even her American friends." One local TV anchor once told Hema, "You don't have just one daughter; you have two." "She has that soft-hearted nature," adds Pam, who speaks of her mother with nonstop admiration. "She's strict, though. People respect her so much."

The second generation of the Potla family works for Hema's Kitchen, with the third not far behind. Pam has always worked alongside her mother at all three locations. Pam's husband, Paul Pritpal, manages Hema's Kitchen II on Clark. Though he's not a staff chef, says Pam,

"He's a good cook. When there's no one there, he cooks." Their eldest son, Rahul, also loves to cook, and he seems destined to take over the family business one day. "We asked him, 'Do you want to take over what Amma has established for so many years?' He said, 'Yes, but I would like to put my style on it.'"

These days, Hema continues to devote much of her time to her church, which is in the village of Katavaram, Andhra Pradesh, 500 kilometers from Hyderabad. "It's a beautiful church," says Hema. "There are so many weddings there, so many baptisms. My oldest sister's grandson, he got married in the church. The pastor was my nephew's father." I asked Hema if she plans on going to India to see the fruits of her labor. "No! I can't even go to Detroit!" she laughed, referring to an invitation she declined to attend a friend's engagement party. She blames her restaurants for keeping her in Chicago, working, 364 days a year—only taking a break for Christmas Day. On a recent Christmas, Hema says, she started to feel restless by evening. She didn't know what to do with herself.

Hema's husband, Sam, said that he was more of a dreamer, and that Hema was the practical one in the marriage. But I think you have to be a bit of a dreamer to come to a foreign country on your own and try to make a living running your own business. Even Sam thought she would go to America and be back in four months. In Chicago, local business owners on Devon predicted that Hema's Kitchen would go out of business in six months. Says Pam of her mother, "One fellow, when he was in India, he just looked at her hand and said, 'Even if you go to a forest, you will make money. You will know how to live.'"

One day, I came to talk with Hema while I was recovering from a stomach virus. Indian food was not on my list. I tried my best to explain why I couldn't eat any of the dishes offered at our usual table. I thought I succeeded, and we continued with our conversation. As I was leaving, Hema stood up, looking up at me with a worried, concerned look on her face.

"You know, you didn't eat anything, and I feel bad for that."

Sourcing Food on Devon

You will not see any distributor trucks pulling up to the restaurants on Devon between Damen and Kedzie, the commercial district dubbed Little India that attracts shoppers from a 300-mile radius. Since opening Hema's Kitchen in West Rogers Park in 1991, Hema has been able to purchase all her spices, meats, produce, and other ingredients within walking distance. While other neighborhoods in Chicago suffer from being in what are known as food deserts, Little India boasts an abundance of grocery stores within just a few blocks.

World Fresh Market, 2434 West Devon Avenue

Well-known for achieving complex depth of flavor in her food, Hema sources her spices from World Fresh Market across the street at 2434 West Devon. World Fresh is owned by the Yassin family, who came to Chicago from Palestine. Hema also buys much of her food from Fresh Farms at 2626 West Devon. Known for its stellar produce selection, Fresh Farms has several locations throughout Chicagoland, each catering to the ethnic makeup of the neighborhood in which it is located. At the Devon location, for example, staff speak English, Hindi, Urdu, Greek, Spanish, and Hebrew.

Hema sources other ingredients from Patel Brothers, an Indian grocery at 2610 West Devon that opened its first location on Devon in 1974, before Little India was established as a neighbhorhood. There are now dozens of Patel Brothers locations around the country. Just a few blocks east is Farm City Meat at 2255 West Devon, Hema's meat vendor since 1991. First-generation owner Fozi Suleiman, who came to the United States in 1971 from Palestine, still mans the counter at this grocery and butcher shop, open since 1985. Suleiman hasn't seen significant changes to the ethnic makeup of the area since 1985; his store has always carried food from all over the world, including Zabiha Halal meats.

The *Check, Please!* Effect

Check, Please! is one of Chicago Public Television station WTTW's highest-rated local programs, attracting thousands of viewers per episode. The show has become so ingrained in Chicago's culture that most locals can probably recite the host's introduction: "Welcome to *Check Please!*, the show where regular people from all over Chicago recommend and review their favorite restaurants."

Restaurants featured on *Check, Please!* typically experience a huge surge in business after their episode airs. Some restaurants have gotten so slammed after being featured on the show that they started referring to a *Check, Please!* effect. Even iconic steakhouses have been known to experience the *Check, Please!* effect. "Gibson's told me their business went through the roof" after their episode aired, said the show's cocreator David Manilow, who expressed disbelief to Gibson's owner upon hearing this news. "He said no, no no, these are all people who have never been here before."

Manilow has heard hundreds of similar stories over the show's run, which began in 2001. Restaurant owners have told Manilow that "they can send their kids to college now" after being featured on the show. But Manilow's favorite story is from Joe Quercia at Freddy's Pizza, an Italian deli and grocery store in Cicero. "On the Saturday after the show, which airs on Friday night, Joe was cooking in the back of the restaurant," recalled Manilow. "A customer called, asking 'hey, how long does it take to get there?' Joe thinks someone is asking, 'how long does it take to get to Cicero?' And Joe says, 'well, where are you?' And he goes, 'well, I'm in line at the alley.' Joe walks outside . . . The line had wrapped around the block!" Now most restaurants know what to expect before agreeing to be on the show. "We have a lot of years, a track record of driving traffic," said Manilow. "It doesn't surprise anybody at this point."

Haryali Chicken

Haryali ("green" in Hindi) chicken is an original dish that Hema Potla created in Chicago. The chicken is cooked in a delicious blend of ground cilantro, green chilies, curry leaves, mint, and coconut.

Ingredients

2 lbs. boneless chicken
2 Tbsp. oil
1 Tbsp. chili powder
1 Tbsp. ground coriander
½ Tbsp. ground cumin

½ tsp. ground turmeric
2 Tbsp. oil
¼ c. half-and-half
Salt to taste

Paste #1: Grind the following ingredients into a smooth paste and set aside:
  ½ c. cilantro
  6 green chilies
  ¼ c. mint
  4 black peppercorns
  ½ c. freshly grated coconut

Paste #2: Grind the following ingredients into a smooth paste and set aside:
  2-inch piece of fresh ginger
  6 cloves garlic
  ½-inch piece of cinnamon stick
  5 cardamom pods

Directions

1. Marinate the chicken in paste #1 for 30 minutes.
2. Meanwhile, heat the oil in a deep pan and sauté paste #2 to a golden brown. When oil oozes from the sides of the paste, add the chili powder, coriander, cumin, and turmeric. Stir for 5 minutes until cooked.
3. Add the marinated chicken to the pan. Stir well, cover, and cook over low heat for about 10–15 minutes. Remove the lid and add the half-and-half. Stir.
4. Keeping the flame low, cook uncovered for another 5–10 minutes, or until the chicken is cooked.
5. Serve immediately over basmati rice.

Aloo Baigan

This popular dish reflects the cuisine of South India, where Hema Potla was born and raised. Aloo baigan is a vegetarian dish that features potatoes and eggplant with grated coconut in a rich curry sauce.

Ingredients

1½ tsp. roasted sesame seeds
1½ tsp. peanuts, lightly sautéed
4 Tbsp. oil
1 lb. Indian eggplant, cut into 1-inch pieces*
½ tsp. cumin seeds
1 small onion, diced
2 green chilies, diced
A few curry leaves
2-inch piece of fresh ginger and 6 cloves of garlic, ground into a paste
¼ tsp. asafetida
1 tsp. chili powder
1 tsp. ground coriander
¼ tsp. ground turmeric
2 medium potatoes, boiled and cut into 1-inch cubes
2 tsp. grated coconut
½ c. chopped coriander leaves (cilantro)
Salt to taste

Directions

1. Grind the sesame seeds and peanuts together.

2. Heat the oil in a pan and fry the eggplant pieces until they are tender. Set them aside.

3. In the same oil, add the cumin. Cook until it begins to pop and sputter.

4. Add the onion and green chilies. Sauté until the onions are golden brown. Add the curry leaves and ginger and garlic paste. Sauté again for two minutes.

5. Add the asafetida, chili powder, coriander, and turmeric. Sauté for one minute.

6. Add the potato cubes. Stir for a minute, until the potatoes are coated.

7. Add the eggplant pieces to the mixture. Stir lightly and cook for 3 more minutes.

8. Add the ground sesame and peanuts and shredded coconut. Mix well. Cover with a lid and let it cook for 3 minutes. Take off the lid, turn off the heat, and add the chopped coriander leaves (cilantro).

9. Serve immediately.

*The eggplant pieces can be covered in salted water for 30–45 minutes then rinsed and patted dry, to avoid the fried eggplant from becoming too greasy.

Eight

NOON O KABAB
King of Kedzie

"It takes a certain group of people to give up everything in one country, move to a strange culture, and . . . open a Persian restaurant in a city where only one or two existed. It takes a lot of courage and management skills, which we had."

—Hamed Mirzamani

Bread and Meat

"My Dad wanted to open this place," explains Mir Naghavi, who opened Noon O Kabab (Farsi for "bread and meat") with his father, Amin, and sister Parvin at 4661 North Kedzie in March 1997. Mir's other sister, Nasrin, joined the business when she came to the United States from Tehran in 2001.

Amin wanted to open a shop where he could sell his well-known pickles and jams. "He was very famous for his jams," says Mir of his late father. "He was making Persian jams all over the world. Unbelievable. I just got involved to start him off. It was meant to be a very casual place. We were only supposed to have ground beef and bread, and then jams and a little bit of sweets and so forth. Unfortunately, we got busy!" he says, laughing. "We had jams and everything, but they vanished years ago. And that's where it all started."

Mir came to the United States from Tehran by himself in 1978 to pursue higher education. "I was an architectural draftsman before I came here," he says. "I wanted to get a degree, and it was very difficult to get into the university in my country." Once in the United States, Mir moved back and forth between Tennessee and Alabama, where he met his wife, Masako. Missing big-city life (Masako is from Tokyo), the couple decided to move to Chicago, where they opened an American fast-food place at Broadway and Addison in 1981. They named it Yellow Submarine as a nod to their shared affection for The Beatles.

Yellow Submarine lasted three years—impressive for any restaurant, especially for first-time restaurateurs in a new city. After their first venture closed, Mir and Masako opened Layly Majnoon, a Persian restaurant at Clark and Touhy. By that time, Mir's father had arrived in Chicago from Tehran and helped out in the kitchen. "He was a great chef," says Mir. Layly Majnoon was in business for about a year when Mir realized that running a restaurant was just too stressful for him. At this point, Mir's mother and sister Parvin had also moved to Chicago from Tehran, and in 1985 the family went into the Persian carpet business. "SIAS Gallery in Evanston, just across the street from Le Peep Restaurant," says Mir. "We were there for a long time. We were quite successful."

With his larger-than-life presence, Mir typically serves as Noon O Kabab's spokesperson. Selling Persian carpets was a "very comfortable business," he remembered. "Not too much stress, that a restaurant normally has." When SIAS closed in 1991, Mir brought his colorful personality and connections in the community to the Nahigian Brothers Galleries, a Persian rug department in the old Marshall Field's. Mir thought he had finally found his niche in Chicago, away from the stressors of running a restaurant—until his father needed help establishing Noon O Kabab, now a fixture in Chicago's Albany Park neighborhood.

Naghavi's Kababs: No Knife Needed

As soon as Noon O Kabab opened in 1997, the Naghavi's kababs, particularly the *koubideh* (ground sirloin with Persian spices), were an immediate hit with the Albany Park neighborhood and beyond. The tiny storefront eatery made it to the *Chicago Tribune's* "Cheap Eats" column in 1998, where it received a four-forks rating from critic William Rice. The exposure from a feature on *Check, Please!* in 2002 resulted in even longer lines for Noon O Kabab's dine-in and carryout business. Demand soon strained the confines of the small kitchen and thirty-five seat dining room. "Customers would pick up their orders and eat them in the old Kentucky Fried Chicken's parking lot next door," says Mir. "We had lines out the door. If I'd been open 24/7, there'd be lines out the door 24/7. Especially after *Check, Please!*" Noon O Kabab's instant success was a mixed blessing: Business flourished from day one, but it took all of the family's resources, and Amin Naghavi's jams never made it past the kitchen.

Chicagoans have been eating kababs as far back as 1893. A *Chicago Sun-Times* article about the Columbian Exposition described "merchants in the hot kabab (sausage) trade" hawking their wares on the Midway Plaisance. Mir explains why Persian food is cooked on kababs: "We Persians do not like the meat to touch the grill. It doesn't matter how hot the grill is; there is always something there that is old, or burnt, or not good for your body. That's why we put most of our food, even salmon, on two-and-a-half foot skewers on open fire." Chefs elevate the skewers above the grill, where it still hits the charcoal flame, but not the grill itself.

The Naghavis' kababs are legendary for being extremely tender, juicy, and perfectly seasoned. No knife is needed. Besides the popular *koubideh*, customers also love the *chenjeh* (ribeye steak), *joujeh* (marinated chicken), shrimp, leg of lamb, and the signature salmon. After Noon O Kabab opened, Mir's customers told him his salmon was the best they'd had anywhere in the world. "I said, 'I don't believe this,'" the chef-owner says. "But then I did go all over the world. We have amazing salmon! We have a lot of compliments on my salmon from very strong restaurants."

Persian food is distinguished from Middle Eastern fare with its more delicate use of spices and unique cooking methods.* Persian rice, or *polo*, for example, is twice cooked. "We cook it to a certain softness, and then we strain all the white starch out," Mir explains. "That's why it's not sticky anymore. Then, we put it in a dry pan, a little bit butter, close the top. It has its own moisture; it cooks in its own steam."

A staple in Persian cuisine, rice is offered several ways at Noon O Kabab—all of the basmati variety. Unique and most popular is *shirin polo*—an exotic combination of white rice, saffron, orange peel marmalade, pistachios, shredded carrots, golden raisins, and barberry, a tiny, tart berry most akin to the cranberry. "They're very small," Mir says of the barberry, which he imports from Iran. "We grill them very lightly. They should not change to black. They're very sour." A strong proponent of balanced food pairings, Mir declares *shirin polo* a great complement to salmon, chicken, and shrimp. *Adass polo* is his suggested pairing with beef. A delicious mix of white rice, lentils, raisins, caramelized onions, saffron, and barberry, the dish is hearty enough to be a meal on its own.

"You'll Never Hear Anyone Else Say This"

When Mir speaks of harmonized food pairings, he is not just concerned about his customer's palates. Rather, he believes that certain ingredients harmonize—or don't harmonize—in the body. He calls it body acceptance. "If you have beef in the body . . . you need to have tomato next to it in your stomach," he explained, asserting that this helps counteract the potential buildup of cholesterol in one's blood. Mir also maintains that dill helps dial down the amount of sugar from rice and that the enzymes in onions help digest rice. "For a long time I never served coffee here," says Mir. "It doesn't work with rice. Coffee is not gonna harmonize, it's not gonna balance." Mir recalled a playful argument with a customer who was denied after-dinner coffee. "I

---

*The country of Iran was known as Persia until 1935. The Islamic Republic of Iran was founded in 1979 after the Iranian Revolution. Iranian is a nationality, while Persian is used in cultural contexts. Iran's official language is Persian, otherwise known as Farsi. Iran is not an Arab nation.

shocked this man. He said, 'Damn Persian guy, give me my coffee!' I said 'not here!' It was friendly, just joking. He was like, 'You're like a soup Nazi! I want my coffee!' I told him, 'We break your habits here. I'm Persian.'" Mir served the man tea.

Customers' emotions drive Mir more than any business owner I've ever met. "As a human, what drives your life is your emotions," he says, emphasizing every syllable with an intense passion that extends to all aspects of his business. "You're not paying attention to it through your food. Very healthy food might not be good for you. You'll never hear anyone else say this," an expression Mir often uses when sharing his beliefs about everything from business to relationships to health to food. "These . . . new chefs, they want to be so fascinating and so creative to my eyes! They wanna mix African diet next to Japanese next to, let's say, Vietnamese next to Persian, and put 'em on the same plate and give it to me. They don't understand that the body works differently. That's why people get sick, even though the food wasn't bad at all, wasn't spoiled. All I worry about here is that my promise to the customer, whether they're coming here for twenty minutes or an entire evening, is they have to be safe emotionally and physically."

Just when I think I have Mir pegged, he'll say something that throws this notion in reverse. "I'm a junk-food junkie," he says, laughing, just seconds after espousing the benefits of food and body acceptance. "I used to stop at Home Depot and get two Polish sausages and a Coke on my way to my job! But my doctor said, 'With your stress, you better stop it.'"

Persian Food: Not Adapted for American Tastes

Many restaurateurs who come to Chicago from other corners of the globe tend to modify their cuisine to suit American palates. Not the Naghavis. Since the restaurant opened in 1997, the menu has been nearly 100 percent authentic Persian food, using spices imported from Iran. Hummus and baba ghanoush are some of the only non-Persian items on the menu. They were added due to their popularity. "All of this," Mir says, making a sweeping gesture across his menu, "can be found in Tehran. Nothing has been modified. Chinese people have to do that. Indian people have to do that. But not Persians, because we are very moderately spiced to begin with. I really have to emphasize on that."

While Persian food may not pack the heat of Sichuan or Indian cuisine, it does possess a depth of flavor when in the hands of talented chefs like the Naghavis. One bite of something as simple as their Persian salad, made with pickled cucumbers, tomatoes, onions, and mint, reveals bursts of flavor and perfect seasoning.

Besides barberries and spices, Noon O Kabab also imports saffron and pomegranates, which are used liberally throughout the menu in dishes such as pomegranate mushrooms and charbroiled chicken wings with pomegranate glaze. Almost everything is made in-house, even the *kashk* (aged dried yogurt) and *bastani* (Persian ice cream, in flavors like fig and saffron). They order their pita bread from Sanabel Bakery down the street but bake their own naan-like breads in larger ovens installed in 2017.

"Our food is very moderately spiced. That's where we separate ourselves with the restaurant. It's coming from very deep in the culture, what we call *erfan*. It's a kind of Sufiism," Mir explains. To spread his message, Mir trademarked the slogan "Food with Persianality" and uses the expression "Perfectly Persian" throughout the restaurant's signage, menu, and marketing materials. His goal, he says, is to "Persianize" diners. One week, after I had feasted several times on Noon O Kabab's succulent kababs, fragrant *polo*, and soothing Persian tea, I did indeed feel . . . calmer. More relaxed. Pampered. Had I been Persianized? I don't know. But I will admit that the gastrointestinal issues I was having at the time disappeared. Perhaps there was something to body acceptance, after all.

Albany Park: "A Wonderful Melting Pot"

Noon O Kabab is in Albany Park on the Northwest Side of Chicago. A tight-knit neighborhood, Albany Park is defined by a high foreign-born population and strong community organizations. The area is roughly bounded by California on the east, the Edens Expressway to the west, Montrose on the south, and Foster on the north (City of Chicago 2015). Ravenswood Manor, a subdivision of Albany Park, was placed on the National Register of Historic Places in 2005, largely due to the Ravenswood Manor Improvement Association's efforts to preserve the local housing stock. One of Ravenswood Manor's most famous residents is former Illinois governor Rod Blagojevich, who was sent to federal prison in 2012 on corruption charges.

The land that is now Albany Park was annexed to the city of Chicago along with the rest of Jefferson Township in 1889. A few years later, a group of investors bought a 640-acre area of land nearby. One of these investors, DeLancy Louderback, named the new region after his hometown of Albany, New York. This helped bring resources such as streetcars to Albany Park as early as 1896 (Neary 2005).

Over the years, Albany Park's population has been a revolving door of different ethnic groups attracted to the affordable housing and business opportunities in the area. Scott Berman, an attorney and president of the Lawrence Avenue Development Corporation, was born and raised in Albany Park. His family owns Super Dawg, the iconic drive-in hot dog joint at Milwaukee and Devon (with a second location in Wheeling, Illinois). He has been closely involved with Albany Park's growth on a personal, political, and professional level since the 1950s.

Many Jewish families, Berman says, moved from overcrowded conditions on Chicago's West Side to Albany Park at the beginning of the twentieth century. After the El was extended to Kimball in 1907, Albany Park's population exploded, going from about 7,000 in 1910 to more than 55,000 in 1930 (Neary 2005). Kimball, Kedzie, and Lawrence became Albany Park's major commercial thoroughfares.

After World War II, Berman explains, the Jewish community left Albany Park all at once. "Not in a white flight manner as in other places around the country, but for two other reasons. One, the G.I. Bill comes and gives soldiers money to buy things in the suburbs. And two, the Edens Expressway, which was then called the Edens Superhighway, was built in the Chicago area. Before the Kennedy, before the Dan Ryan, before the Eisenhower, first was the Edens Superhighway. Hence the growth of Skokie and the Edens Expressway communities."

The Jewish community's exodus represented a dramatic change in Albany Park's demographics. When Berman attended Volta Elementary at 4950 North Avers from 1956 to 1964, he remembers, the student body was almost 100 percent Jewish. When Berman's younger sister graduated Volta in 1975, she was one of only five Jewish students at the school. "From 1964 to 1975," Berman says, "Volta went from a thousand Jewish kids to five Jewish kids."

After the Jewish population left, the vacant apartments and houses left behind quickly filled up with Korean families, the next wave of immigrants that came to Albany Park. "The surrounding housing community is strong and it always has been," says Berman. But the surrounding business areas suffered, reaching a 45 percent vacancy rate in 1975, the same year Berman joined the North River Commission and became the organization's first lawyer. Berman and his team brought commercial investments into the area such as beautification projects, SBA loans, and building façade improvements. By 1980, the retail vacancy rate in Albany Park was down to zero. "By doing . . . public improvements and private improvements and working with the landlords to fill their businesses, and working with the residents to bring in their ethnic businesses, we were able to fill in. And this is one person telling another, block by block. That's why Lawrence Avenue has been so successful all these years. This is all North River Commission and Lawrence Avenue Development Corporation, which is the nonprofit economic development arm of the North River Commission."

The neighborhood's Korean population grew during the period of 1978 to 1990, according to Berman. Lawrence Avenue from Kedzie to Pulaski became the honorary Seoul Drive to acknowledge the Korean-owned shops and restaurants. By the early 1990s, however, the majority of the Korean population moved out of Albany Park, and new immigrants from the Middle East, Latin America, and Central and Eastern Europe moved in. "We wind up being this wonderful melting pot of Eastern and Central Europe, Middle Eastern, Hispanic . . . and everybody gets along incredibly well," says Berman. "The store owners meet each other, so our Chamber of Commerce is very active and has meetings where all these different ethnic groups come, and tell their friends to come."

The Kedzie Retail District

Noon O Kabab is located in the Kedzie retail district, which runs a half mile between Montrose and Lawrence. Since the 1980s, this strip has gradually become a destination for those seeking Middle Eastern restaurants, bakeries, and grocery stores.

Louie Alipoulos is the second-generation owner of Andy's Fruit Ranch at 4733 North Kedzie. His family opened their store, originally a fruit stand, in 1979. "The area was a food desert" back then, says Alipoulos. Andy's started carrying products for the neighborhood's growing Arab population in the late 1980s. Customers started driving in from out of state to purchase hard-to-find Middle Eastern products and groceries.

Al-Khayam Bakery and Feyrous Bakery appeared in Albany Park in the 1980s to cater to the burgeoning Middle Eastern community, and both were still going strong on Kedzie more than thirty years later. Salam Restaurant opened at 4634 North Kedzie in the Metro Plaza in 1989, eight years before Noon O Kabab. Salam has changed hands over the years, most recently to the Blan family, who has owned the Metro Plaza since the mid-1990s. The Blans, who are from Jordan, doubled Salam's space in 2009 to keep up with their growing business. Nazareth Sweets first opened as a small bakery in the Metro Plaza in the 1990s, moving to a larger space at Lawrence and Kedzie in 2005 as business increased (operations have since moved to Elston Avenue).

Nasrin Naghavi's son, Hamed Mirzamani, moved to the United States from Tehran with his family in 2001. Noon O Kabab and Salam Restaurant were the only other Middle Eastern restaurants nearby, he remembers. "It was just Noon O Kabab and Salam back then," he says. "But now people are more comfortable opening restaurants in this area." People like Joseph Abraham, who opened Semiramis in 2003 at 4639 North Kedzie, just across the El tracks from Noon O Kabab. Chef-owner Abraham's authentic Lebanese food soon made the Chicago Michelin Guide and brought more and more people to the Kedzie retail district.

By 2016, there were several groceries on Kedzie besides Andy's that carried Middle Eastern baked goods, spices, groceries, and Zabiha Halal meats.* Andy's continues to track the neighborhood's demo-

*Halal meats come from animals permissible and slaughtered per Islamic law. A portion of Noon O Kabob's menu is halal.

graphics and alters its products accordingly. In 2016, they were carrying "some" Philippine products, more and more Mexican and Asian foodstuffs, and a growing number of items from Eastern Europe.

Though the Kedzie retail district is dominated by Middle Eastern businesses, the surrounding area, like many neighborhoods on Chicago's Northwest Side, has been attracting a growing number of Hispanic residents. According to the 2010 U.S. Census, of Albany Park's 52,000 residents, about 50 percent are Hispanic, 29 percent are white, 14 percent are Asian (mostly Korean), and 4 percent are African-American.

"It's a destination restaurant," says Mir of Noon O Kabab, which attracts Persians from all over Chicagoland. "We are not a neighborhood restaurant."

Few Persian Restaurants in Chicago

Though there are more and more Middle Eastern restaurants opening in the Kedzie retail district and throughout Chicagoland, there are less than a handful of Persian restaurants in Chicago that have stood the test of time. As a lifelong Chicagoland resident, I have only seen a few: Noon O Kabab, Pars Cove, and Reza's.

Brothers Reza and Gholam Toulabi first opened Reza's at 5255 North Clark in 1984. Two locations followed in Oak Brook and River North, the latter of which is now closed. My first encounters with Persian food were at Reza's. I remember taking home Styrofoam containers stuffed with leftover dill rice, the portions too daunting to consume in one meal. Their charbroiled kababs were so simple, yet so delicious and flavorful.

When I lived on the North Side, I discovered Pars Cove at 435 West Diversey Parkway. Opened by Max Pars in 1976, Pars Cove is the city's oldest Persian restaurant, established before the second wave of Iranian immigrants arrived to Chicago or gentrification efforts came to Lincoln Park. I still find Pars Cove's subterranean-level, dimly lit dining room and tucked-away location exotic and intriguing.

Mir's nephew Hamed offers insight as to why so few Persian restaurants exist in Chicago. "Our numbers are low in Chicago," he says of the city's Persian population, "even including the ones who reside in the suburbs. But to compete with what's in California . . . We actually have a name for it: we call it Tehran-geles. And we have a high population of Persians in Toronto. We call that Tehran-to. So we have these little areas where there's high populations of Persians. Chicago, I don't think we have one."

There are strong Arab populations throughout Chicago, especially Lebanese and Palestinian. Though Iran is a close neighbor with the twenty-two countries that form the League of Arab States, Persians are not Arabs. Defined by a common language, Persians speak Farsi, not Arabic. Persians are often referred to as Middle Eastern, but even this is a loose term that includes Arab nations and, sometimes, Iran, Turkey, and Israel. As far as I can tell, there does not seem to be a concentrated Persian population anywhere in Chicagoland.

"I don't want anybody to mix up Persian food with Middle Eastern," Mir says. "That doesn't mean disrespect, but it's a different culture.

We are a very moderate culture. An acceptance culture. That is expressed through our food and our art."

The first meaningful wave of Persian immigration to the United States started in the 1950s and lasted until the 1970s. Medical professionals largely made up this group. The second wave occurred after the 1979 Iranian Revolution, when mostly educated, middle-class Iranians fled the country (Akbari and Khounani 2005, 43).

Noon O Kabab's clientele, says Mir, is about 10 to 20 percent Persian—quite impressive when you consider Chicago's relatively small Persian population, estimated at the turn of the twenty-first century at about

6,000–10,000 in the city and 30,000 in the metropolitan area (Kessler 2005). Though Chicago's Persian population might be smaller than other major cities', Chicago boasts a strong, supportive community that celebrates Iranian heritage. Nowruz, the traditional Iranian festival of life, was first celebrated in the State Building in downtown Chicago in 1994. In 1995, Illinois governor Jim Edgar proclaimed March 21 Iranian Heritage Day in Illinois. The University of Chicago's Oriental Museum holds one of the largest Persian archaeological collections, and their library's Persian section is one of the largest Persian collections in the United States (Akbari and Khounani 2005, 23, 30).

"There's a huge risk of having a Persian restaurant" in Chicago, says Hamed. "Our population is very low in the city of Chicago. We have to not only impress the Persians, but also the other ethnicities to try our food. For example, there's a restaurant called Taste of Peru at 6545 North Clark. For them to attract me as a Persian to go in there and actually like the food, takes a lot. It takes word of mouth, takes advertising. I'm now a constant customer of theirs. The same goes for us. Having this restaurant, with how powerful it is, and having Reza's, who is more powerful, and having all these other restaurants come in . . . It's hard to come in and say, hey, this is a new Persian restaurant, let's see if it's gonna work out. It would be a difficult task. We all have good food. There is something else that Persians care about, and that is, can we do that to our neighbor? Should we do something that would hurt our neighbor? If there is a car dealership owned by a Persian, should I open up another car dealership when a Persian already owns one and potentially hurt him? There's a loyalty that you see among Persians. Hence these things added all together could be why we have so few Persian restaurants in Chicago."

The Accidental Restaurateur

Noon O Kabab has occupied three different addresses on Kedzie at one time or another—all within the same block. In 1997, they opened their main dining room at 4661 North Kedzie, which was expanded from thirty-five to eighty seats in 2006.

In 2008, they took over the building two doors south at 4651 North Kedzie to accommodate their flourishing carryout and catering busi-

The original Noon O Kabab eat-in dining and carryout and catering businesses were in two separate buildings, at 4661 and 4651 North Kedzie. Noon O Kabab now operates in one building at 4701 North Kedzie.

ness. Marie Farhat was hired as Noon O Kabab's catering manager the same year. "Every time someone picked up an order, they had to walk through a busy dining room," says Farhat. "Mir didn't want to keep disturbing everybody in the dining room, so he got this building." "My landlord promised to sell me the building; he never did," says Mir of 4651 North Kedzie, which had just a few small tables for self-serve customers interested in a quick bite.*

In desperate need to expand, the Naghavis started renovating the building at 4701 North Kedzie, a former Kentucky Fried Chicken, in 2013. In fall 2016, they opened a fast-casual restaurant in the 3,500-foot, remodeled space, which accommodates 75 self-serve diners and carryout orders. The dining room at 4661 North Kedzie was also bursting at the seams, so the Naghavis broke ground on the same lot at

---

*Noon O Kabab's first catering and carryout business at 4651 N. Kedzie was in a building right next to the El's crossing gates at street level. Contradicting the very nature of Chicago's El, or system of elevated train tracks, the northern stretch of the CTA's Brown Line train roared past Noon O Kabab to the Kedzie stop across the street. This section of the Brown line was completed in 1907 when the land was still privately owned. Developers built it at grade, as it was cheaper than building tracks above the street. Now called the Ravenswood line, this part of the El runs at grade in the alleyways between Leland and Eastwood and has six stops: Spaulding, Kedzie, Albany, Sacramento, Francisco, and Rockwell.

4701 North Kedzie in October 2015 to build 3,500 square feet of additional space. The new, octagon-shaped dining room, which only serves dinner, connects to the fast-casual side through a hallway and finally enables Noon O Kabab to combine its catering, carryout, dine-in, delivery, and self-serve businesses under one roof, with one kitchen, at one address (4661 North Kedzie now serves as a special event space). "I knew I could be doing twice the business that I was doing," says Mir.

The expansion to one, larger space at 4701 North Kedzie was long overdue. "A lot of restaurants on Kedzie have closed down over the years," says Farhat. "But Noon O Kabab has grown pretty much every year." The family also has a third location, NOK, an eighty-seat fast-casual spot, which opened in 2013 at 6075 North Milwaukee.

"I'm still growing," says Mir, referring to Noon O Kabab's small empire in the Kedzie Retail District, where he's been dubbed the "mayor" by Alderman Deb Mell. "Hopefully to the point that I'm done building!" the accidental restaurateur says, laughing. "For twenty years, I keep building."

While grateful for Noon O Kabab's instant success and consistent growth, Mir often seems to accept his lot as a restaurateur reluctantly. "I didn't mean to open a restaurant at all," he says. "I know that people think that becoming successful is a challenge. But the actual challenge comes after you are successful, because you have more employees, you have more concern, you are more stressed out . . ."

"We are the family that does not cut corners," says Hamed, who reveres his uncle and late grandfather and considers both as mentors in his life. "That's something that I realized. I remember once back in 2008, 2009, when my uncle opened the catering kitchen, I noticed he was buying heavy-duty plastic forks and spoons. And when I compared the prices to the light ones, you could see a substantial difference in price. So I asked him, 'Why don't you just buy the cheaper ones? They're going to get thrown away anyway.' And he told me, 'Customer satisfaction. You want to be able to pick up the meat and the rice and not have the plastic fork bend. You want to be able to rip the meat apart.' I was thinking, let's save money, let's save money.

"There have been times when we have brought spices from Iran because they were not available due to sanctions," Hamed continues. "I remember my mom bringing a little bit of spices to the restaurant, because we were having a hard time finding them. We could have easily gone to the supermarket and found an alternative source, but simply for the fact that it wasn't Persian, or that it could result in a different taste, wasn't satisfying to my family. We don't cut corners. Now I realize that if you cut corners, the customers will notice it, and they won't come. We have people who come here maybe ten to fifteen times a month. It's the loyalty they have in us, and we have in them. We go above and beyond. It's more than food for my family. It's really the experience of the culture. Do I see myself someday potentially running this business? Yes. I could see myself. But at the same time, I believe I have so much more to learn."

"Mir is a very kind man," says Farhat about her employer. "He's nice to his employees. I believe that he does the best he can for everybody." But Mir rejects labels such as "boss" or "employee." "Never a server, I always say a partner," he emphasizes. "I kept telling everybody, you are not a server, you're not a bartender, you're not a cook, you're all priceless humans. Don't *ever* respect me," he says. "If you want to say hello to me, you can say hello to me. If you don't want to say hello to me, don't say hello. I want you to understand the reason that we're talking to each other." As is typical, Mir pivots from intense to light-hearted at the drop of a hat. "I'm not uptight or anything. I believe in Harley Davidson choppers, I believe in 1100HP cars. I took many rabbis dancing. I believe in salsa, cha cha cha dancing. I've become a five minutes clown. I like to joke around, have fun, with every table, with every soul, with every person. I push other people to have fun.

"If I had more time, I would have done more things and failed more," he says, laughing. "I fail at so many things because of my personality. I can never finish anything, you know what I'm saying? I challenge myself. It's a difficult business. This restaurant business is a difficult business. It's been a fantastic journey with my family. My dad was a great cook. Both sisters are amazing cooks. I learned a lot about myself. Very hard business. I'm still growing."

Amin Naghavi, a Local Legend

Amin Naghavi, Noon O Kabab's cofounder and family patriarch, came to Chicago from Iran in 1982. According to his children, he didn't like to drive. So he walked. When the Naghavi family ran SIAS Galleries, a Persian carpet business in Evanston, Amin would walk all the way from downtown Evanston to downtown Chicago and back—twice a week.

As he walked, he would stop along the way, engaging in deep conversations with people he met from all over the world about geography, politics, literature—all topics on which he was expert. Amin delivered food and flowers to several people a day, people who became his friends—for a day, a year, a lifetime. Until the year before his health started to fail, said Mir, his father would still walk several miles, eat a piece of pizza, and walk back.

Already imposing with his 6′4″ frame, Amin was a bodybuilder in his younger days. Said Hamed Mirzamani, "My grandpa, when he was healthy enough, would walk six, seven miles before 9 A.M., and this was five years" before he passed away at the age of ninety-five. "When he was my age, he had eight-packs. And I look at myself and I'm like, 'what happened to me? Where did these genes go?'"

Amin also had a tough side that served the family business well. "He was definitely a respected man in this restaurant," said Hamed. "Every time he walked in here, all the staff got in order. He brought his management skills from Iran and deployed them here. And it simply worked."

"He was so kind," said Mir. "Very pure hearted. Fearless. I was very close to him. We started this business because of a passion that we have for people."

Kash-Ke-Bademjan (Pureed Eggplant)

Persian dishes vary from family to family, region to region. This is Parvin Naghavi's recipe, which is commonly served as an appetizer at Noon O Kabab. The Naghavis cover the eggplant with oil while frying, then press the eggplant overnight to help drain it. To prepare this at home, simply use less oil to suit your taste, or about 3 tablespoons. If you cannot find kashk, *Greek yogurt can be used as a substitute.*

Ingredients

3 large eggplants
7 Spanish onions
Vegetable oil (up to 10 oz.)
1 Tbsp. salt
2 Tbsp. turmeric

1 Tbsp. black pepper
3 c. (24 oz.) water
2 c. (16 oz.) liquid aged yogurt (*kashk*), available in Middle Eastern groceries
2 Tbsp. dried mint (do not use boiled mint)

Directions

1. Peel the skin off the eggplants. Dice eggplant into small pieces, about 1½ inches. Lightly fry in a pan with vegetable oil until brown, about 3 minutes each side. Set aside.

2. Chop 6 of the Spanish onions. In a separate pan, fry onions in vegetable oil until brown, or for a few minutes. Add the salt, half of the turmeric, and the pepper. Stir to combine.

3. Add the fried eggplant to the onion mixture. Stir.

4. Slowly add all of the water and *kashk* to the pan, stirring slowly and continuously until mixture is combined. For a smoother consistency, you may use a hand blender.

5. Chop the remaining Spanish onion. Pan fry until golden brown and caramelized. Add the remaining turmeric and stir until completely absorbed. Remove pan from heat. After about two minutes, add the dried mint. Stir to combine.

6. Add the caramelized onion to the eggplant and onion mixture. Stir.

7. Serve immediately.

Optional: Set aside a small amount of the caramelized onions and spoon on top of the *kash-ke-bademjan*.

ACKNOWLEDGMENTS

Heartfelt thanks to Gianna Mosser, editor in chief at Northwestern University Press, for championing this work since its early stages. It's every writer's dream to receive an immediate response from an editor who understands and encourages your vision with such heart and enthusiasm. I would also like to thank Harvey Young for building the Second to None series and promoting my favorite topic—Chicago, a city with a bottomless well of incredible stories.

I would also like to extend my sincere gratitude to the entire team at Northwestern University Press; it is an honor to work with such a talented, fun, hard-working group. Special thanks to my editor, Nathan MacBrien, who toiled over every word and detail with me. And to JD Wilson, Greta Bennion, and the marketing and sales team—your passion and enthusiasm for this project strengthens my commitment to make sure these inspiring stories reach as many readers as possible.

Thank you, also, to early readers Mindi Rowland, Suzanne Sonnier, and Susan Blumberg, who ensured that I was on the right track. And to John Rohsenow and Scott Berman, who were invaluable resources along the way. Thanks, also, to the Kooky Cookbook Club and NUP staff who lovingly prepared the recipes in this book and provided valuable feedback.

Much love and gratitude also go to friends and family who encouraged me to pursue this work from the beginning. Your support means the world to me.

Most of all, I am grateful to the Huey, DiBuono, Gutierrez, Liakouras, Figueroa, Hebal, Potla, Naghavi, and Mirzamani families. While I was writing and researching this book, they all experienced a lot of life.

Family weddings. Loss. Some closed their doors. One experienced a tragic fire. Others built and opened new locations. Yet each and every one gave me their time, their stories, their recipes, and their trust. For this, I am truly grateful.

Chapter 1. Won Kow: The Old Guard of Chinatown

Bronson, Bennet, Joe Chiu, and Chuimei Ho. 2011. *Chinatown in Chicago: A Visitor's Guide to Its History and Architecture*. Chicago: Chinatown Museum Foundation.

Chen, Joyce. 1962. *The Joyce Chen Cook Book*. Philadelphia and New York: J. B. Lippincott Co.

Chinatown Museum Foundation. 2005. *Chinese in Chicago 1870–1945*. Images of America series. Edited by Chuimei Ho and Soo Lon Moy. Charleston, S.C.: Arcadia Publishing.

Eldredge, Barbara. 2016. "Chinese Investment in U.S. Real Estate Still Booming, Says Report." *Curbed*, May 18. http://www.curbed.com/2016/5/18/11691870/chinese-investment-real-estate-united-states.

Gourse, Leslie. 1988. "Dim Sum Has Come a Long Way, from Esoteric to Mass Popularity." *Chicago Tribune*, March 13.

Lau, Yvonne M. 2006. "Chicago's Chinese Americans: From Chinatown and Beyond." In *The New Chicago: A Social and Cultural Analysis*, edited by John P. Koval et al., 168–81. Philadelphia: Temple University Press.

Lee, Raymond B. 2015. *Growing Up in Chicago's Chinatown: The Stories of Raymond Lee*. Chicago: Chinese American Museum of Chicago.

Loring, Kay. 1970. "Where to Dine Christmas Day." *Chicago Tribune*, December 20.

Rohsenow, John. 2003. "Chinese Language Use in Chicagoland." In *Ethnolinguistic Chicago: Language and Literacy in the City's Neighborhoods*, edited by Marcia Farr, 320–55. Mahwah, N.J.: Lawrence Erlbaum Associates.

Spiers, Katherine. 2015. "Tiki's Hollywood Origins and the Woman Behind It All." *Serious Eats*, March 24. http://www.seriouseats.com/2015/03/tiki-history-hollywood-cocktails-food-sunny-sund.html.

U.S. Census Bureau. 2014. United States Census 2000, 2010–14. Data available at www.census.gov.

Chapter 2. Tufano's Vernon Park Tap: A Long Lifeline in Little Italy

Candeloro, Dominic. 1995. "Chicago's Italians: A Survey of the Ethnic Factor, 1850–1990." In *Ethnic Chicago: A Multicultural Portrait*, 4th ed., edited by Melvin G. Holli and Peter d'A. Jones, 229–59. Grand Rapids, Mich.: Wm. B. Eerdmans Publishing Co.

Catrambone, Kathy, and Ellen Shubart. 2007. *Taylor Street: Chicago's Little Italy*. Images of America series. Charleston, S.C.: Arcadia Publishing.

Chapter 3. The Gutiérrez Family: A Phoenix in Pilsen

Casuso, Jorge, and Eduardo Camacho. 1995. "Latino Chicago." In *Ethnic Chicago: A Multicultural Portrait*, 4th ed., edited by Melvin G. Holli and Peter d'A. Jones, 346–77. Grand Rapids, Mich.: Wm. B. Eerdmans Publishing Co.

Diaz, Tom. 2009. *No Boundaries: Transnational Latino Gangs and American Law Enforcement*. Ann Arbor: University of Michigan Press.

Osorio, Jose M. 2015. "Nuevo Léon Restaurant Destroyed in Extra-Alarm Fire in Pilsen." *Chicago Tribune*, December 2. Video.

Pero, Peter N. 2011. *Chicago's Pilsen Neighborhood*. Images of America series. Charleston, S.C.: Arcadia Publishing.

Pew Research Center. 2016. "Hispanic Population and Origin in Select U.S. Metropolitan Areas." Accessed November 12, 2016. http://www .pewhispanic.org/interactives/hispanic-population-in-select-u-s -metropolitan-areas/.

Pridmore, Jay. 1991. "The Soul of Pilsen: Day of the Dead Brings Community to Life." *Chicago Tribune*, October 25.

Saclarides, Kathryn. 2009. "Selling Chicago as a Global City: Redevelopment and Ethnic Neighborhoods." *Advocates' Forum*. http://ssa.uchicago.edu/ advocates-forum-2009.

U.S. Census Bureau. United States Census 2010.

WTTW Chicago. 2013. "Chicago Time Machine: Battle of the Viaduct." Accessed November 12, 2016. http://interactive.wttw.com/timemachine/ red-bridge.

Chapter 4. The Parthenon: An Anchor in Greektown

Blei, Norbert. 2003. "Dance with Me Petros!" In *Chi Town*, 319–26. Evanston, Ill.: Northwestern University Press. First published in 1990 by Ellis Press.

Ganakos, Alexa. 2005. *Greektown Chicago: Its History—Its Recipes*. St. Louis: G. Bradley Publishing.

Gekas, George J. 1991. *Opaa! Greek Cooking Chicago Style!* Los Angeles: Bonus Books.

Johnson, Charles J. 2014. "Parthenon Blazes a Trail." *Chicago Tribune*, September 8.

Louik/Schneider & Associates. 1996. "City of Chicago Near West Redevelopment Project Area Tax Increment Finance Program: Redevelopment Plan and Project." May 30. http://www.cityofchicago.org/dam/city/depts /dcd/tif/plans/T_032_NearWestRDP.pdf.

Mourtoupalas, Connie. 2014. "Reaching for the American Dream: The Legacy of Greek Immigration in America." Chicago: National Hellenic Museum.

Ori, Ryan. 2015. "Greektown Buildings Sell for Almost $30 Million." *Crain's Chicago Business*, July 1. http://www.chicagobusiness.com/realestate/ 20150701/CRED03/150639978/greektown-buildings-sell-for-almost-30 -million.

Segal, David. 2009. "The Gyro's History Unfolds." *New York Times*, July 14. http://www.nytimes.com/2009/07/15/dining/15gyro.html.

Stagg, Camille J. 2008. *The Parthenon Cookbook: Great Mediterranean Recipes from the Heart of Chicago's Greektown*. Evanston, Ill.: Surrey Books.

Chapter 5. Borinquen: Home of the *Jibaro*

Chicago Sun-Times. 1966. "Crowd Burns 2 Police Cars." June 18.

Chicago Tribune. 2007. "Places to See in Chicago Before You Die—Revised." July 17.

Cintrón, Ralph, Maura Toro-Morn, Ivis García Zambrana, and Elizabeth Scott. 2012. "60 Years of Migration: Puerto Ricans in Chicagoland." The Puerto Rican Agenda. http://puertoricanchicago.org/wp/wp-content/uploads/ 2015/05/Full_report.pdf.

Cohn, D'Vera, Eileen Patten, and Mark Hugo Lopez. 2014. "Puerto Rican Population Declines on Island, Grows on U.S. Mainland." *Pew Research Center*, August 11. http://www.pewhispanic.org/2014/08/11/puerto-rican -population-declines-on-island-grows-on-u-s-mainland/.

Cruz, Wilfredo. 2004. *Puerto Rican Chicago*. Images of America series. Charleston, S.C.: Arcadia Publishing.

Eng, Monica. 2000. "Cheap Eats. Plantain Variations: Starchy Banana Relative Stars at Puerto Rican Restaurant." *Chicago Tribune*, August 23.

———. 2003. "Saga of a Sandwich." *Chicago Tribune*, June 18.

Fernandez, Lilia. 2012. *Brown in the Windy City: Mexicans and Puerto Ricans in Postwar Chicago*. Chicago: The University of Chicago Press.

Chapter 6. Red Apple Buffet: A Pillar in Polonia

Biemer, John. 2004. "Community's Devotion Helps St. Hyacinth Become Basilica." *Chicago Tribune*, January 2.

Dukes, Jesse. 2015. "Can Chicago Brag about the Size of Its Polish Population?" WBEZ 91.5 Chicago, October 26. Accessed October 21, 2016.
https://www.wbez.org/shows/curious-city/can-chicago-brag-about-the
-size-of-its-polish-population/ef8c74cd-8835-4eb7-8e81-11203e78fc2d.

Erdmans, Mary Patrice. 2006. "New Chicago Polonia: Urban and Suburban." In
The New Chicago: A Social and Cultural Analysis, edited by John P. Koval
et al., 115–27. Philadelphia: Temple University Press.

Granacki, Victoria. 2004. *Chicago's Polish Downtown*. Images of America series. Charleston, S.C.: Arcadia Publishing.

Kantowicz, Edward R. 1995. "Polish Chicago: Survival through Solidarity." In
Ethnic Chicago: A Multicultural Portrait, 4th ed., edited by Melvin G. Holli
and Peter d'A. Jones, 173–198. Grand Rapids, Mich.: Wm. B. Eerdmans
Publishing Co.

Kaplan, Jacob, Daniel Pogorzelski, Rob Reid, and Elisa Addlesperger. 2014.
Avondale and Chicago's Polish Village. Images of America series. Charleston, S.C.: Arcadia Publishing.

Zurawski, Joseph W. 2007. *Polish Chicago: Our History, Our Recipes*. St. Louis:
G. Bradley Publishing.

Chapter 7. Hema's Kitchen: Doyenne of Devon

Bruno, Pat. 2008. "Bruno's Quick Bites." *Chicago Sun-Times*, September 12.

Day, Jacque E., and Jamie Wirsbinski Santoro. 2008. *West Ridge*. Images of
America series. Charleston, S.C.: Arcadia Publishing.

Indo-American Center. 2003. *Asian Indians of Chicago*. Images of America
series. Charleston, S.C.: Arcadia Publishing.

Rangaswamy, P. 1995. "Asian Indians in Chicago: Growth and Change in a
Model Minority." In *Ethnic Chicago: A Multicultural Portrait*, 4th ed., edit-
ed by Melvin G. Holli and Peter d'A. Jones, 438–62. Grand Rapids, Mich.:
Wm. B. Eerdmans Publishing Co.

Samors, Neal, Mary Jo Doyle, Martin Lewin, and Michael Williams. 2001.
*Chicago's Far North Side: An Illustrated History of Rogers Park and West
Ridge*. Chicago: The Rogers Park/West Ridge Historical Society.

U.S. Census Bureau. 2012. "The Asian Population: 2010." 2010 Census Briefs.
March. https://www.census.gov/prod/cen2010/briefs/c2010br-11.pdf.

Chapter 8. Noon O Kabab: King of Kedzie

Akbari, Hamid, and Azar Khounani. 2005. *Iranians in Chicagoland*. Images of
America series. Charleston, S.C.: Arcadia Publishing.

City of Chicago. 2015. "Chicago Maps Community Areas: Albany Park." June.
Accessed August 23, 2016. http://www.cityofchicago.org/content

/dam/city/depts/doit/general/GIS/Chicago_Maps/Community_Areas/
CA_ALBANY_PARK.pdf.

Kessler, James S. 2005. "Iranians." In *The Electronic Encyclopedia of Chicago*.
Chicago: Chicago Historical Society. Accessed September 1, 2016. http://
www.encyclopedia.chicagohistory.org/pages/650.html.

Neary, Timothy B. 2005. "Albany Park." In *The Electronic Encyclopedia of
Chicago*. Chicago: Chicago Historical Society. Accessed August 10, 2016.
http://www.encyclopedia.chicagohistory.org/pages/36.html.

Rice, William. 2008. "Cheap Eats. Perfectly Persian." *Chicago Tribune*, April 8.

Second to None: Chicago Stories
celebrates the authenticity of a city
brimming with rich narratives and
untold histories. Spotlighting original,
unique, and rarely explored stories,
Second to None unveils a new and
significant layer to Chicago's big-
shouldered literary landscape.

Harvey Young, series editor